Introduction

365 Easy One-Dish Recipes is all about helping everyone who cooks do it in less time and really enjoy the results.

The importance of family meals is well known. Family meals do much to keep families together, to enrich lives and to instil healthy values and habits.

365 Easy One-Dish Recipes makes it easy to plan, to cook and to serve delicious dishes to family and friends. All the ingredients are readily available in your own pantry, refrigerator or the familiar shelves in your local supermarket. Meals are easy when you start with easy recipes and an easy plan.

Most recipes do not need anything to go with them. Others are even better with a simple salad and bread from your own refrigerator or the supermarket. And there is a BONUS section in this book with desserts!

Cooking is one of life's simple pleasures. And these recipes make it easy to enjoy quality time with people you care about.

Contents

Beautiful Brunches 7

Casseroles, Breakfast Sandwiches, Coffee Cakes and French Toast

Super Salads 23

Veggies, Fruits, Pasta, Greens and Meats

Snappy Sandwiches 57

Hot, Cold, Open-Face, Veggies and Meats

Savoury Soups & Stews 77

Cheeses, Beans, Veggies, Greens and Meats

Big-Time Beef 109

Baked, Grilled, Fried and Cooked Slow and Easy

Contents

Dedication

With a mission of helping you bring family and friends to the table, this book aims to make family meals and cooking for friends simple, easy and delicious.

We recognise the importance of a meal together as a means of building family bonds with memories and traditions that will be treasured for a lifetime. It is an opportunity to sit down with each other and share more than food.

This cookbook is dedicated with gratitude and respect to all those who show their love with homecooked meals, bringing family and friends to the table.

More and more statistical studies are finding that family meals play a significant role in childhood development. Children who eat with their families four or more nights per week are healthier, attain higher marks at school, score higher on aptitude tests and are less likely to have problems with drugs.

Beautiful Brunches

Casseroles, Breakfast Sandwiches, Coffee Cakes and French Toast

Beautiful Brunches Contents

Breakfast Frittata

2 medium zucchini, diced and
　drained
1 cup (70 g) finely diced fresh
　mushrooms
Canola oil
2 ripe avocados, peeled and cubed
5 eggs
1½ cups (160 g) shredded Swiss
　cheese

- Cook zucchini and mushrooms in
  large frypan with a little oil over
  medium heat for 4 to 5 minutes
  or just until tender. Remove from
  heat and sprinkle with a little salt
  and pepper.

- Place cubed avocado over top of
  vegetable mixture. Beat eggs and
  about 1 cup (250 ml) water or
  milk until frothy and pour over
  ingredients in frypan.

- Return frypan to medium heat,
  cover and cook for 5minutes
  or until eggs set. Top with
  cheese, then cover and cook for
  additional minute or just until
  cheese melts. Cut into wedges to
  serve. Serves 6.

Corned Beef Hash 'n' Eggs

1 425-g (15-ounce) can corned
　beef, shredded
1 310-g (11-ounce) can
　corn, drained
4 eggs
¾ cup (205 g) chilli sauce

- Preheat oven to 190° C (375° F).

- Spread corned beef in sprayed
  23-cm (9-inch) pie dish and
  spoon corn over beef.

- With large spoon, make
  4 depressions in corn and break
  1 egg in each depression. Spoon
  chilli sauce over top of eggs.

- Bake for 20 minutes or until
  eggs set. Serves 4.

Bacon & Eggs, Anyone?

2 potatoes, peeled and cubed
¼ cup (60 g) plus
   3 tablespoons (45 g) butter,
   melted
¼ cup (30 g) flour
455 g (1 pint)
   unthickened cream
450 g (16 ounces)
   shredded cheddar
   cheese
1 teaspoon dried
   Italian seasoning
12 eggs, hard-boiled and
   sliced
450 g (1 pound) bacon, cooked
   and slightly crumbled
1½ cups (90 g) breadcrumbs

- Cook potatoes in salted water in saucepan just until tender, but do not overcook. Drain well.

- In separate saucepan, melt ¼ cup (60 g) butter and stir in flour. Cook, stirring constantly, 1 minute or until smooth.

- Gradually add cream and cook over medium heat, stirring constantly, until sauce thickens. Add cheddar cheese, Italian seasoning, and a little salt and white pepper, stirring constantly, until cheese melts. Remove from heat.

- Layer half egg slices, half bacon and half cheese sauce in sprayed 23 x 33-cm (9 x 13-inch) baking dish. Spoon potatoes over cheese sauce and top with remaining egg slices, bacon and cheese sauce.

- Combine breadcrumbs and 3 tablespoons (45 g) melted butter in bowl. Sprinkle over top of casserole. Cover and refrigerate overnight.

- When ready to bake, preheat oven to 175° C (350° F).

- Before baking, remove casserole from refrigerator and let stand for about 20 minutes. Uncover and bake for 30 minutes. Serves 8 to 10.

Breakfast Bake

This is a favourite for overnight guests or special enough for Christmas morning.

450 g (1 pound) hot salami, cooked and crumbled
1 cup (115 g) shredded cheddar cheese
1 cup (120 g) scone mix
5 eggs, slightly beaten
2 cups (500 ml) milk

- Preheat oven to 175° C (350° F).

- Place cooked, crumbled salami in sprayed 23 x 33-cm (9 x 13-inch) baking dish and sprinkle with cheese.

- Combine scone mix with a little salt and eggs in bowl and beat well. Add milk and stir until fairly smooth. Pour over sausage mixture.

- Bake for 35 minutes. You can mix this up the night before cooking and refrigerate. To cook the next morning, add 5 minutes to cooking time. Serves 6.

Crabmeat Quiche

3 eggs, beaten
230 g (8 ounces) sour cream
1 170-g (6-ounce) can crabmeat, rinsed, drained, flaked
½ cup (55 g) shredded Swiss cheese
1 sheet refrigerated shortcrust pastry

- Preheat oven to 175° C (350° F).

- Combine eggs and sour cream in bowl. Blend in crabmeat and cheese and add a little salt and pepper.

- Line a greased 23-cm (9-inch) pie dish with pastry and pour egg mixture into dish.

- Bake for 35 minutes. Serves 6.

Fiesta Eggs

450 g (1 pound) salami
½ green capsicum, chopped
½ red capsicum, chopped
3 spring onions, chopped
1 280-g (10-ounce) can tomatoes
50 g (2 ounces) green chilli, diced
½ cup (130 g) hot, chunky salsa
½ cup (65 g) cubed processed
** cheese**
10 eggs, slightly beaten
½ cup (120 g) sour cream
⅔ cup (165 ml) milk

- Preheat oven to 160° C (325° F).

- Slowly brown salami, capsicums and onions in frypan. Spoon mixture onto paper towels, drain and set aside.

- Dry frypan with more paper towels, pour tomatoes, green chillies, salsa and cheese into frypan and cook, stirring constantly, only until cheese melts. Remove from heat.

- Beat eggs, 1½ teaspoons salt, sour cream and milk in bowl and fold in salami mixture and tomato-cheese mixture. Transfer to sprayed 18 x 28-cm (7 x 11-inch) baking dish.

- Bake for about 25 minutes or until centre is set. Serves 8.

Chiffon Cheese Soufflé

Wow! This soufflé is great! It is light and fluffy, but still very rich.

12 slices white bread with crusts trimmed
280 g (10 ounces) processed cheese spread, softened
6 eggs, beaten
3 cups (750 ml) milk
¾ cup (170 g) butter, melted

- Cut each bread slice into 4 triangles. Place dab of cheese on each triangle and place triangles evenly in layers in sprayed 23 x 33-cm (9 x 13-inch) baking dish. (You could make this in a soufflé dish if you have one.)

- Combine eggs, milk, butter and a little salt and pepper in bowl. Pour over layers. Cover and refrigerate for 8 hours.

- Remove from refrigerator 10 to 15 minutes before baking.

- When ready to bake, preheat oven to 175° C (350° F).

- Bake for 1 hour. Serves 8.

Breakfast Tortillas

¾ cup (120 g) chopped onion
¼ cup (60 g) butter
¼ cup (30 g) flour
¾ cup (175 ml) milk
500 ml (1 pint) unthickened
    cream
1 200-g (7-ounce) jar chopped
    green chillies
10 eggs
3 avocados
8 20-cm (8-inch) flour tortillas
230 g (8 ounces) shredded Colby
    cheese

- Preheat oven to 175° C (350° F).

- Sauté onion in butter in large frypan. Stir in flour, cook on low 1 minute and stir constantly. Add milk and cream, cook on medium heat and stir constantly until mixture thickens.

- Add green chillies and ½ to 1 teaspoon each of salt and pepper. Remove sauce from heat and set aside.

- In separate frypan, scramble eggs lightly and remove from heat.

- Mash avocados and sprinkle with a little salt in small bowl.

- Lay out tortillas on bench and place 2 tablespoons (30 ml) sauce, one-eighth of eggs and one-eighth of avocados on each tortilla. Roll and place seam-side down on sprayed 23 x 33-cm (9 x 13-inch) baking dish. Spoon remaining sauce over tortillas.

- Cover and bake for about 25 minutes or just until tortillas are hot and bubbly. Remove from oven, sprinkle cheese over top and return to oven for about 10 minutes. When serving, top each tortilla with a dab of salsa, if desired. Serves 8.

TIP: To remove tortillas from baking pan, always use a long, wide spatula with holes in it so that the tortillas do not break up.

English Muffin Breakfast Sandwich

6 eggs
230 g (8 ounces) bacon slices,
   halved
6 English muffins,
   halved and toasted
6 cheese slices

- Scramble eggs in frypan over medium heat and stir often. Season according to taste.

- Cook bacon in separate frypan or in the microwave. Spoon egg mixture onto bottom of muffin, add cheese slice, bacon and muffin top. Serves 6.

Mexican Breakfast Eggs

4 tablespoons (60 g) butter
9 eggs
3 tablespoons (45 ml) milk
5 tablespoons (75 g) salsa
1 cup (55 g) crushed corn chips

- Melt butter in frypan. Beat eggs in bowl and add milk and salsa.

- Pour into frypan and stir until eggs are lightly cooked.

- Stir in corn chips and serve hot. Serves 6.

Quick Breakfast Sandwiches

Wouldn't the kids love to say they had sandwiches for breakfast! What a cool Mum!

8 slices white bread*
Butter, softened
2 cups (280 g) cooked, finely chopped ham
1 cup (110 g) shredded Swiss cheese
3 eggs, beaten
1⅔ cups (415 ml) milk
1 tablespoon (10 g) minced onion flakes
1 teaspoon mustard

- Trim crusts off bread slices. Spread butter on 1 side of each slice of bread. Place 4 slices in sprayed 20-cm (8-inch) square baking pan.

- Top bread slices with chopped ham and remaining bread slices, buttered-side up. Sprinkle with shredded Swiss cheese.

- Combine eggs, milk, onion flakes, mustard and about ½ teaspoon salt in bowl and mix well. Slowly pour over bread slices. Cover and refrigerate overnight or at least 8 hours.

- When ready to bake, preheat oven to 160° C (325° F).

- Remove baking pan from refrigerator about 10 minutes before cooking. Bake for 30 minutes or until centre sets. To serve, cut into 4 sandwiches. Serves 4.

*TIP: Use toast slices, not thin sandwich slices.

Sunrise Eggs

6 eggs
2 cups (500 ml) milk
450 g (1 pound) salami, cooked
and browned
¾ cup (85 g) shredded processed
cheese
6 slices white bread,
trimmed and cubed

- Preheat oven to 175° C (350° F).

- Beat eggs in bowl and add milk, salami and cheese. Pour over bread and mix well.

- Pour into sprayed 23 x 33-cm (9 x 13-inch) baking pan and cover with foil.

- Bake for 20 minutes. Remove foil and turn oven up to 190° C (375° F) and bake for additional 10 minutes. Serves 6.

Eggs in a Basket

2 425-g (15-ounce) cans corned
beef
6 eggs
¼ cup (30 g) seasoned
breadcrumbs
Butter

- Preheat oven to 160° C (325° F).

- Spread corned beef evenly in sprayed 18 x 28-cm (7 x 11-inch) baking dish. Press bottom of ½ cup (125 ml) measuring cup into meat to make 6 impressions.

- Break 1 egg into each impression. Sprinkle a spoonful of breadcrumbs over each egg and top with a dot of butter. Bake for 20 to 25 minutes or until eggs are as firm as desired. Serves 6.

Overnight Breakfast

This is French toast the easy way and it's not just for guests! The kids will love it too.

7 cups (700 g) French bread, cut into small cubes and bottom crust removed
¾ cup (85 g) chopped pecans
85 g (3 ounces) cream cheese, softened
4 tablespoons (60 g) sugar
230 g (8 ounces) pouring cream
½ cup (125 ml) real maple syrup
6 eggs, slightly beaten
1 teaspoon vanilla
½ teaspoon ground cinnamon

- Place cubed bread in sprayed 23 x 33-cm (9 x 13-inch) baking dish and press down gently. Sprinkle with pecans. Beat cream cheese and sugar in bowl until fluffy and gradually mix in cream and syrup.

- In separate bowl, whisk eggs, vanilla, cinnamon and about ½ teaspoon salt and fold into cream cheese-cream mixture. Slowly pour this mixture evenly over bread. Cover and refrigerate overnight.

- When ready to bake, preheat oven to 175° C (350° F).

- Remove from refrigerator 20 minutes before baking. Cover and bake for 30 minutes or until centre sets and top is golden brown. To serve, cut into squares and serve with maple syrup. Serves 8.

Heavenly Eggs for the Saints

Butter, to taste
1 slice bread
1 mozzarella cheese slice
1 egg
1 precooked bacon slice, heated

- Preheat oven to 175° C (350° F).

- Butter slice of bread and place buttered-side down into baking dish. Place cheese slice over bread.

- Separate egg and add pinch of salt to egg white in bowl and beat until stiff.

- Pile egg white on cheese and make nest in top. Slip egg yolk into each nest and bake for 20 minutes. Serve immediately.

- Cut cooked bacon in half and lay pieces over egg like a cross. Serve immediately. Makes 1.

TIP: If you want to make more, just multiply the ingredients.

Orange French Toast

1 egg, beaten
½ cup (125 ml) orange juice
5 slices raisin bread
1 cup (105 g) crushed crackers
2 tablespoons (30 g) butter

- Combine egg and orange juice in bowl.

- Dip each slice of raisin bread in egg mixture and then in cracker crumbs.

- Fry in butter in frypan until brown. Serves 5.

Breakfast Cinnamon Cake

⅔ cup (150 g) packed brown sugar
1 tablespoon (15 g) grated
    orange peel
560 g (20 ounces) scone mix
2 teaspoons cinnamon
3 tablespoons (45 g) brown
    caster sugar

- Preheat oven to 190° C (375° F).

- Combine brown sugar and orange peel in small bowl.

- Add cinnamon and caster sugar to scone mix, then prepare scone dough according to the packet directions. Cut dough into eighths and coat each piece with cooking spray.

- Dip in sugar-orange mixture and arrange evenly in sprayed 25-cm (10-inch) ring pan. Gently press down on each. Bake for 15 minutes or until light brown and risen.

- Cool slightly in pan. Invert serving plate on top of pan, hold plate and pan together with oven mitts and invert. Remove pan and serve warm. Serves 6.

Cherry-Pecan Porridge

2 cups (160 g) porridge oats
½ cup (60 g) dried cherries,
    chopped
½ cup (110 g) packed brown
    sugar
¼ cup (60 g) butter, softened
½ teaspoon ground
    cinnamon
½ cup (55 g) chopped pecans,
    toasted

- Cook porridge in saucepan.

- Combine cherries, brown sugar, butter and cinnamon in bowl. Stir into cooked porridge.

- Spoon into individual serving bowls and sprinkle toasted pecans over top of each serving. Serve 6.

Croissant French Toast with Strawberry Syrup

4 large day-old croissants
¾ cup (175 ml) unthickened
  cream
2 large eggs
1 teaspoon vanilla
¼ cup (60 ml) butter

- Slice croissants in half lengthwise. Whisk cream, eggs and vanilla in shallow bowl. Heat 1 tablespoon (15 g) butter in large frypan.

- Dip croissant halves into egg mixture and coat well. Cook for about 2 minutes, 4 croissant halves at a time, turn and cook on both sides until light brown.

- Repeat procedure with remaining butter and croissant halves.

Strawberry Syrup:

700 g (1 quart) fresh
  strawberries, sliced
¾ cup (150 g) sugar
¼ cup (60 ml) orange juice

- Combine all ingredients in saucepan and let stand for 30 minutes.

- Cook over medium-low heat, stirring occasionally for 5 to 8 minutes. Serve warm over croissant toast. Serves 4.

No-Mess Oven Pancakes

⅔ cup (80 g) flour
⅔ cup (165 ml) milk
¼ cup (50 g) sugar
5 large eggs, beaten
Canola oil
Maple syrup or fresh
    strawberries

- Preheat oven to 220° C (425° F).

- Combine flour, milk, sugar and eggs in bowl. Place a little oil on large baking tray and rub oil to cover whole surface. Place in oven for 5 minutes to heat.

- Pour pancake mixture onto pan to make several pancakes. Bake for about 18 minutes or until puffy and golden.

- Serve with maple syrup and fresh berries. Serves 3.

Breakfast Shake

1 banana, cut into chunks
1 mango, peeled and cubed
1½ cups (375 ml) pineapple juice
    or orange juice, chilled
230 g (8 ounces) vanilla yoghurt

- Process banana slices, mango, juice and yoghurt in blender until smooth. Scrape sides of blender and mix. Serve immediately. Serves 2.

Super Salads

Veggies, Fruits, Pasta, Greens and Meats

Super Salads Contents

Zesty Bean Salad

1 425-g (15-ounce) can kidney
  beans
1 425-g (15-ounce) can borlotti
  beans
450 g (16 ounces) frozen corn,
  thawed and drained
1 red onion, chopped
1 green capsicum, seeded and
  chopped
1 200-g (7-ounce) can chopped
  green chillies
2 cups (280 g) cubed deli ham

- Rinse and drain kidney beans
  and borlotti beans and place in
  salad bowl.

- Add corn, onion, capsicum,
  green chillies and ham and mix
  well.

Dressing:

230 g (8 ounces) ranch dressing
2 tablespoons (30 ml) lemon juice

- Pour ranch dressing into small
  bowl and stir in lemon juice.

- Pour over salad and toss.
  Refrigerate for several hours
  before serving for flavours to
  blend. Serves 4.

*Keep your salads crisp for longer by chilling
the salad plates or serving bowl.*

Easy Vegetable Salad

1 head cauliflower
1 head broccoli
280 g (10 ounces) frozen green
    peas, thawed
2 sticks celery, diagonally
    sliced
1 bunch spring onions, sliced
2 cups (280 g) cubed deli ham

- Wash and drain cauliflower and broccoli and break into florets.

- Place in large bowl. Add peas, celery, spring onions and ham; toss well.

Dressing:

2 cups (450 g) mayonnaise
¼ cup (50 g) sugar
1 tablespoon (15 ml) white
    vinegar
1 cup (115 g) shredded
    mozzarella cheese

- Combine all dressing ingredients in bowl and pour over vegetables and toss.

- Refrigerate for several hours before serving. Serves 8.

Lettuce or greens to make a salad are not required.
For a quick, 'straight-out-of-the-refrigerator' salad,
mix broccoli, cauliflower, celery, cucumbers, tomatoes,
green beans and anything else you find on the shelves
that might work. Pour in your favourite dressing and toss.

Greens and Rice Salad

280 g (10 ounces) mixed baby
    salad greens
2 cups (370 g) cooked rice, chilled
650 g (23 ounces) mandarin
    segments
½ cup (65 g) thinly sliced
    spring onions, chilled
230 g (8 ounces) Italian
    salad dressing
1 teaspoon ground cumin
1 avocado, peeled and well
    mashed

- Combine salad greens, rice, mandarins and spring onions in salad bowl.

- Combine salad dressing, cumin, avocado, and ½ teaspoon each of salt and pepper in jar with lid. Pour about half the dressing over salad and toss. Add more as needed. Serves 6.

Harmony Salad

2 heads red lettuce, torn
650 g (23 ounces) mandarin
    segments
2 avocados, peeled and cubed
1 red onion, sliced
230 g (8 ounces) red wine
    vinaigrette dressing
¼ cup (30 g) sunflower seeds

- Place lettuce, mandarins, avocados and onion slices in salad bowl and refrigerate.

- Drizzle about half salad dressing over salad, toss, using more if needed. Sprinkle sunflower seeds over top of salad. Serves 4.

Fruit and Greens Delight

560 g (20 ounces) radicchio
    salad mix
2 golden delicious
    apples, cored and
    cut into wedges
1¼ cups (170 g) crumbled
    blue cheese
⅔ cup (85 g) chopped walnuts
⅔ cup (170 g) apple sauce
⅓ cup (85 ml) olive oil
⅓ cup (85 ml) cider vinegar
1 tablespoon (15 g) Dijon-style
    mustard

- Combine salad mix, apples, blue cheese and walnuts into a salad bowl.

- Combine apple sauce, oil, vinegar and mustard into a small bowl and mix well. Toss with salad. Serves 4.

TIP: If you slice the apples several minutes before serving, sprinkle 1 tablespoon (15 ml) lemon juice over them and toss so they will not turn dark.

Radicchio has a deep red leaf with white ribs and looks similar to red cabbage. Small amounts add a nice accent to other salad greens.

Pasta Toss

230 g (8 ounces) bow-tie pasta
1 tablespoon (15 ml) olive oil
2 cups (245 g) diagonally sliced
   carrots
2 cups (140 g) broccoli florets
1 red capsicum
1 yellow capsicum
2 cups (280 g) cooked, cubed
   ham
¾ cup (175 ml) creamy Italian
   salad dressing
2 tablespoons (30 ml) balsamic
   vinegar
1 tablespoon (15 g) sugar
½ teaspoon salt
½ teaspoon pepper

- Cook pasta according to package directions. Drain, add olive oil and cool.

- Add carrots, broccoli, capsicums and ham.

- Combine salad dressing, vinegar, sugar, salt and pepper into a bowl and pour over vegetables and toss.

- Refrigerate for several hours before serving. Serves 6.

The main difference between the names of plain pasta are the shapes. While the taste is the same, certain shapes of pasta work better in certain recipes. The more complex the design, the more sauce will stick to the pasta.

Super Summer Salad Supreme

150 g (⅓ pound) roast beef,
    cubed
1 425-g (15-ounce) can 3-bean
    salad, chilled and drained
230 g (8 ounces) mozzarella
    cheese, cubed
280 g (10 ounces) mixed
    salad greens
Italian dressing

- Lightly toss beef, 3-bean
  salad and cheese in large salad
  bowl. Add greens and pour in
  just enough salad dressing to
  moisten greens. Serves 6 to 8.

*TIP: You can substitute turkey or
    ham for beef and Swiss cheese
    for mozzarella.*

Pasta and Lemon Pea Salad

450 g (1 pound) bow-tie pasta
280 g (10 ounces) frozen baby
    green peas, thawed
½ cup (110 g) mayonnaise
2 tablespoons (30 ml) lemon juice
½ cup (125 ml) pouring cream
2 cups (280 g) cooked, cubed
    ham

- Cook pasta according to package
  directions. Add peas during
  last 2 minutes of cooking time.
  Drain pasta and peas, rinse in
  cold water and drain again.

- Transfer to large salad bowl.
  Combine mayonnaise with
  lemon juice, 1 teaspoon salt and
  a little pepper and stir in cream
  and ham.

- Fold mayonnaise mixture into
  pasta and peas and toss to coat
  well. Refrigerate for several
  hours before serving. Serves 6.

Gourmet Couscous Salad

280 g (10 ounces) couscous
1 teaspoon chicken stock powder
2 tomatoes, coarsely
chopped
2 zucchini, coarsely
chopped
4 spring onions, sliced
1 cup (140 g) cubed deli turkey
1 cup (135 g) crumbled feta
cheese
1 tablespoon (15 ml) lemon juice
¼ cup (60 ml) olive oil
½ teaspoon dried basil
½ teaspoon black pepper

- Cook couscous according to package directions, but do not use butter. Stir in chicken stock.

- Combine tomatoes, zucchini, spring onions, turkey and couscous in salad bowl.

- Combine lemon juice, oil, basil and pepper into a jar with lid and shake until they blend well.

- When ready to serve, add feta cheese, pour dressing over salad and toss. Refrigerate. Serves 6.

Couscous is a fine, round Middle Eastern pasta that is often thought of as a grain. It can be served as a breakfast cereal, dressed as a salad, sweetened for a dessert or eaten as a side dish.

Italian Salad

280 g (10 ounces) mixed salad greens
1 cup (115 g) shredded mozzarella cheese
60 g (2 ounces) sliced black olives
1 425-g (15-ounce) can cannellini beans, rinsed and drained
230 g (8 ounces) Italian dressing

- Combine greens, cheese, olives and cannellini beans in salad bowl. Toss with salad dressing.

- Serve with Italian bread and cheeses. Serves 6.

Toss the Greens

280 g (10 ounces) mixed salad greens
1½ cups (225 g) halved cherry tomatoes
1 cucumber, sliced
1 red onion, sliced in rings
450 g (1 pound) seasoned, cooked chicken breasts, cut into strips
Italian salad dressing
Lots of black pepper
¼ teaspoon cayenne pepper

- Combine dressing, black pepper and cayenne pepper into a bowl.

- Combine greens, tomatoes, cucumber and onion rings into a large salad bowl and toss. When ready to serve, toss with salad dressing.

- Arrange salad on individual salad plates, top with strips of chicken and sprinkle with seasoned black pepper and cayenne pepper. Serves 6 to 8.

Rainbow Pasta Salad

**450 g (16 ounces)
tri-colour spiral pasta
1 red capsicum, thinly sliced
1 yellow capsicum,
thinly sliced
4 small zucchini with
peel, sliced
3 sticks celery, sliced
diagonally
1 cup (140 g) cooked, chopped
ham
Lettuce
Breadsticks
1 400-g (14-ounce) can
sweetened condensed milk
1 cup (250 ml) white vinegar
1¼ cups (280 g) mayonnaise
2 teaspoons seasoned
pepper**

- Cook pasta according to package directions. Rinse in cold water and drain well. Combine pasta, capsicums, zucchini, celery and ham in large bowl.

- Combine sweetened condensed milk, vinegar, mayonnaise and seasoned pepper in small bowl.

- Pour half dressing over salad, using more if needed. Toss well, cover and refrigerate overnight.

- Serve over bed of lettuce with breadsticks. Serves 6 to 8.

Chunky Egg Salad

12 eggs, hard-boiled and
    quartered
1 tablespoon (10 g) sun-dried
    tomato pesto
⅓ cup (75 g) mayonnaise
2 sticks celery, sliced
½ cup (65 g) sliced, stuffed
    green olives
Lettuce leaves
Crackers

• Place all ingredients in salad
  bowl and add a little salt and
  pepper.

• Gently toss and serve over bed
  of lettuce leaves with crackers.
  Serves 4.

TIP: This is also great stuffed
    in a hollowed-out tomato,
    capsicum or melon. And
    if you're really in a hurry, just
    put it between 2 slices
    of dark bread.

Spinach Salad

280 g (10 ounces) baby
    spinach
1 cup (165 g) sliced
    strawberries
85 g (3 ounces) slivered almonds,
    toasted
½ cup (70 g) crumbled feta
    cheese
1 cup (140 g) cooked, shredded
    turkey breast
½ cup (100 g) sugar
¼ cup (60 ml) white wine vinegar
⅓ cup (85 ml) olive oil
2 teaspoons poppy seeds

• Combine spinach, strawberries,
  almonds, feta cheese and turkey
  into a salad bowl.

• Combine sugar, vinegar, oil and
  poppy seeds into a bowl and toss
  with spinach mixture. Serves 6.

Super Summer Salad

280 g (10 ounces) risoni pasta
280 g (10 ounces) frozen broccoli florets, thawed
280 g (10 ounces) frozen green beans, thawed
1 340-g (12-ounce) tin baby corn, drained
2 cups (280 g) cooked, cubed ham
1 teaspoon salt
230 g (8 ounces) sweet-and-sour sauce
2 tablespoons (30 ml) olive oil

- Cook pasta in large saucepan according to package directions. Stir in broccoli and green beans 5 minutes before pasta is done.

- Boil and cook for an additional 5 minutes. Drain well. Transfer pasta and vegetables to salad bowl and add corn and ham.

- Sprinkle with salt, pour on sweet-and-sour sauce and olive oil and toss. Serves 8.

In some countries, risoni are known as 'orzo' which means 'barley'.

Chicken Caesar Salad

4 boneless, skinless chicken
    breast halves, grilled
280 g (10 ounces)
    cos lettuce
½ cup (50 g) grated parmesan
    cheese
1 cup (40 g) seasoned croutons
¾ cup (175 ml) Caesar or Italian
    dressing

- Cut chicken breasts into strips. Combine chicken, lettuce, cheese and croutons in large bowl.

- When ready to serve, toss with salad dressing. Serves 8.

Colourful Salad Toss

450 g (16 ounces) baby spinach,
    stems removed
1 small head
    cauliflower, cut
    into small florets
1 red capsicum,
    seeded and cut in strips
¾ cup (90 g) whole walnuts
½ cup (65 g) toasted
    sunflower seeds
2 cups (280 g) cooked,
    chopped ham
Berry vinaigrette

- Combine spinach, cauliflower, capsicum strips, walnuts, sunflower seeds and ham and a generous amount of salt in large salad bowl.

- Toss with strawberry or raspberry vinaigrette salad dressing. Serves 8.

After-Christmas Salad

**560 g (20 ounces)
  cos lettuce**
**2½–3 cups (350–420 g) cooked,
  sliced turkey**
**1 230-g (8-ounce) tin baby
  corn, quartered**
2 tomatoes, chopped
**230 g (8 ounces) shredded
  Colby cheese**
⅔ cup (150 g) mayonnaise
⅔ cup (175 g) salsa
¼ cup (60 ml) cider vinegar
2 tablespoons (30 g) sugar

- Combine cos lettuce, turkey, baby corn, tomatoes and cheese in large salad bowl.

- Combine mayonnaise, salsa, vinegar and sugar into a bowl and mix well.

- When ready to serve, sprinkle on a little salt and pepper, pour dressing over salad and toss to coat well. Serves 8.

TIP: If you want to make this leftover dish an even 'bigger and better' salad, just add some black olives, red onion, borlotti beans or cooked bacon.

Fiesta Holiday Salad

This is great for leftover chicken or turkey!

280 g (10 ounces) torn cos lettuce
3 cups (420 g) cooked, diced chicken or turkey
1 425-g (15-ounce) can borlotti beans, rinsed and drained
2 tomatoes, quartered
⅔ cup (150 g) mayonnaise
¾ cup (200 g) prepared salsa

- Combine lettuce, meat, beans and tomatoes in large salad bowl.

- Combine mayonnaise and salsa.

- When ready to serve, spoon dressing over salad and toss. If you like, a sliced red onion can be added to salad. Serves 8.

TIP: For a little extra touch, you might sprinkle crumbled bacon over top of salad.

Washing and storing lettuce properly will make a big difference to how long it will stay salad-fresh. Remove any bruised, wilted or brown-edged pieces. Separate leaves and wash under cold running water. Use a salad spinner to dry the lettuce and break large pieces to fit in the spinner. Layer dry leaves between paper towels and store in a resealable plastic bag. It should keep for 5 to 7 days. When ready to serve green salad, tear your fresh lettuce and toss with ingredients at the last minute.

Beefy Green Salad

150 g (⅓ pound) roast beef
1 425-g (15-ounce) can 3-bean
    mix, chilled and drained
230 g (½ pound) mozzarella
    cheese, cubed
230 g (8 ounces) mixed
    salad greens
Salad dressing

* Cut beef into thin strips. Lightly
  toss beef, 3-bean mix and cheese
  in large salad bowl. Pour in
  just enough salad dressing to
  moisten greens. Serves 8.

*TIP: You can substitute turkey or
    ham for beef and Swiss cheese
    for mozzarella.*

Borlotti Bean Chicken Salad

3–4 boneless, skinless
    chicken breast halves,
    cooked, cubed
1 425-g (15-ounce) can borlotti
    beans, drained
1 bunch spring onions,
    chopped
1 cup (100 g) chopped celery
¾ cup (175 ml) virgin olive oil
¼ cup (60 ml) lemon juice
2 teaspoons Dijon-style
    mustard
2 teaspoons ground cumin

* Combine chicken, beans, spring
  onions and celery in bowl.

* Combine oil, juice, mustard and
  cumin into a bowl and mix well.

* Pour dressing over salad, toss
  and refrigerate. Serves 6.

Beef and Bean Salad

340 g (¾ pound) roast
   beef, cut in strips
2 425-g (15-ounce) cans
   kidney beans,
   rinsed and drained
1 cup (160 g) chopped onion
1 cup (100 g) chopped celery
3 eggs, hard-boiled,
   chopped
Lettuce
½ cup (110 g) mayonnaise
2 tablespoons (30 g) chilli salsa
¼ cup (70 g) tomato sauce
¼ cup (60 g) sweet pickle relish
2 tablespoons (30 ml) olive oil

- Combine beef strips, beans, onion, celery and eggs in salad bowl.

- Combine mayonnaise, salsa, tomato sauce, pickle relish and oil in bowl and mix well.

- Spoon over beef and bean mixture and toss. Refrigerate for several hours before serving.

- Rather than serving in salad bowl, shred lettuce onto serving plate and serve salad over lettuce. Serves 8.

Fruited Pork Salad Lunch

280 g (10 ounces) salad greens
2 cups (300 g) halved, seedless
  green grapes
1 cup (165 g) fresh strawberries
1 cup (155 g) refrigerated ruby
  grapefruit segments
½–¾ pound (230–340 g) pork
  tenderloin, cooked,
  thinly sliced and chilled
¼ cup (60 ml) pink
  grapefruit juice
2 tablespoons (30 ml) red wine
  vinegar
2 tablespoons (30 ml) oil
1 teaspoon poppy seeds
2 teaspoons honey

- Toss salad mix, green grapes, strawberries and grapefruit segments in salad bowl. Arrange salad on individual plates and place tenderloin slices over top.

- Mix grapefruit, vinegar, oil, poppy seeds and honey into a bowl and pour dressing over top of salads. Serves 8.

Grilled Chicken with Coleslaw

1 1.4-kg (3-pound) chicken, quartered
3 tablespoons (45 ml) olive oil
⅔ cup (165 ml) bottled barbecue sauce
¼ cup (55 g) mayonnaise
3 tablespoons (45 ml) cider vinegar
2 tablespoons (30 ml) sugar
350 g (12 ounces) coleslaw vegetable mix

• Brush chicken quarters with olive oil and sprinkle with a little salt and pepper.

• Grill for 30 to 35 minutes and turn once or twice until juices run clear when thigh part is pierced and meat thermometer registers 75° C (170° F) when inserted into chicken.

• Brush with barbecue sauce and grill just until sauce browns, but do not char.

• Combine mayonnaise, vinegar and sugar in bowl and mix well.

• Spoon over coleslaw vegetables and toss. Refrigerate until ready to serve. Serves 6.

About 80% of the sodium in our diets is from commercial, processed foods. By preparing our own foods, we can control the amount of sodium we eat.

Strawberry and Chicken Salad

450 g (1 pound) boneless, skinless chicken breast halves
Olive oil
280 g (10 ounces) spring greens mix
450 g (1 pint) fresh strawberries, sliced
½ cup (45 g) chopped walnuts
¾ cup (255 g) honey
⅔ cup (165 ml) red wine vinegar
1 tablespoon (15 ml) soy sauce
½ teaspoon ground ginger

- Cut chicken into strips and place in large frypan with a little oil. Cook on medium-high heat for about 10 minutes and stir occasionally.

- While chicken cooks, combine honey, vinegar, soy sauce and ginger into a bowl and mix well.

- After chicken strips cook for 10 minutes, pour ½ cup (125 ml) dressing into frypan with chicken and cook for an additional 2 minutes or until liquid evaporates.

- In separate bowl, combine spring greens mix, strawberries and walnuts, pour on remaining dressing and toss. Top with chicken strips. Serves 6.

Hawaiian Chicken Salad

3 cups (420 g) cooked, diced
    chicken breasts
1 570-g (20-ounce) can
    pineapple pieces,
    well-drained
1 cup (150 g) halved red grapes
1 cup (100 g) chopped celery
1 large banana
¾ cup (170 g) mayonnaise
½ cup (120 ml) lime
    dressing
½ cup (50 g) salted peanuts

- Combine chicken, pineapple, grapes and celery in bowl and toss. Cover and refrigerate.

- Combine mayonnaise, lime dressing and a sprinkle of salt in bowl.

- When ready to serve, slice bananas and add to salad.

- Top with mayonnaise-lime dressing and toss. Just before serving, sprinkle peanuts over top of salad. Serves 8.

Peanuts contain healthy monounsaturated fats as well as vitamin E, folic acid, magnesium, copper, fibre and plant proteins. They are naturally cholesterol-free, help to control cholesterol levels and have almost none of the bad fats.

Barbecue Chicken Salad

Here's a quickie with that 'it-takes-a-long-time' flavour.

¾ cup (175 ml) ranch dressing
3 tablespoons (45 ml) barbecue sauce
2 tablespoons (30 ml) salsa
3 boneless, skinless chicken breast halves, grilled
280 g (10 ounces) cos lettuce
1 425-g (15-ounce) can borlotti beans, rinsed and drained
12–15 cherry tomatoes

- Combine ranch dressing, barbecue sauce and salsa into a bowl. Refrigerate and set aside.

- Cut chicken breasts in strips and heat in oven just enough to warm thoroughly.

- Place chicken strips, cut-up lettuce, beans and cherry tomatoes in bowl.

- Toss enough dressing with salad to lightly coat. Serves 8.

TIP: The next time you grill, just grill some extra chicken breasts and freeze them to use for this dish. Or if you don't have time to grill chicken, just use roast chicken from the supermarket.

Apple and Walnut Chicken Salad

3–4 boneless, skinless chicken breast halves, cooked and cubed
2 tart green apples, peeled and chopped
½ cup (75 g) chopped pitted dates
1 cup (100 g) finely chopped celery
½ cup (45 g) chopped walnuts
⅓ cup (80 g) sour cream
⅓ cup (80 g) mayonnaise
1 tablespoon (15 ml) lemon juice

- Combine chicken, apples, dates and celery in bowl.

- Preheat oven to 150° C (300° F).

- Toast walnuts for 10 minutes.

- Combine sour cream, mayonnaise and lemon juice in bowl and mix well. Add walnuts.

- Pour dressing over chicken salad and toss. Refrigerate. Serves 8.

How many times during our childhoods did we hear the adage, 'An apple a day keeps the doctor away'. As it turns out, the apple is a very nutritious food. Apples contain vitamin C plus many other antioxidants, which are cancer fighters.

Tarragon-Chicken Salad

1 cup (110 g) chopped pecans
3–4 boneless, skinless
   chicken breast halves,
   cooked and cubed
1 cup (100 g) chopped celery
¾ cup (90 g) peeled, chopped
   cucumbers
⅔ cup (150 g) mayonnaise
1 tablespoon (15 ml) lemon juice
2 tablespoons (30 ml) tarragon
   vinegar*
1¼ teaspoons crumbled,
   dried tarragon

- Preheat oven to 150° C (300° F).

- Place pecans in shallow pan and toast for 10 minutes.

- Combine chicken, celery and cucumbers in bowl.

- Combine mayonnaise, lemon juice, vinegar and tarragon into a bowl and mix well.

- When ready to serve, toss with chicken mixture and add pecans. Serves 8.

TIP: If you can't find tarragon vinegar, use white wine vinegar instead.

To chop is to cut into small, irregular pieces about ½ cm in size.

Southwestern Chicken Salad

4 cups (560 g) cubed, cooked
   chicken breasts
1 425-g (15-ounce) can borlotti
   beans, drained
¾ red onion, chopped
½ red capsicum, chopped
½ yellow capsicum, chopped
¼ cup (5 g) chopped fresh
   coriander
½ cup (120 g) sour cream
¼ cup (55 g) mayonnaise
½ teaspoon garlic powder
1 jalapeno chilli, seeded and
   finely chopped
1 teaspoon lime juice
½ cup (65 g) pine nuts, toasted
Lettuce

- Combine chicken, beans, onion, capsicums and coriander in large bowl.

- In separate bowl, whisk sour cream and mayonnaise.

- Stir in garlic powder, jalapeno chilli and lime juice and add to chicken. Add a little salt and pepper and toss.

- Refrigerate for at least 1 hour. Just before serving, toss in pine nuts. Serve on bed of lettuce. Serves 8.

To quickly chop an onion, slice off the stem and root ends and remove peel. Halve the onion from top to root end. Place each onion half flat side down and make ½-cm vertical slices. Holding the vertical slices together, cut ½-cm horizontal slices. There you go!

Mexican Chicken Salad

3–4 boneless, skinless
  chicken breast halves,
  cooked, cubed
1 425-g (15-ounce) can green
  peas, drained
1 red capsicum, seeded and
  diced
1 green capsicum,
  seeded and diced
1 cup (100 g) chopped celery
1½ cups (360 g) sour cream
2 tablespoons (35 g) chilli sauce
2 teaspoons ground cumin
1 small bunch coriander,
  minced

- Combine all ingredients in bowl and serve with dressing.

- For dressing combine sour cream, chilli sauce, cumin and coriander into a bowl and add a little salt and pepper.

- Pour over chicken salad and toss. Refrigerate before serving. Serves 8.

Spinach and Turkey Salad Supper

450 g (16 ounces)
  baby spinach
⅓ cup (40 g) whole walnuts
⅓ cup (40 g) dried cranberries
2 red delicious apples
  with peel, sliced
340 g (¾ pound) cooked
  turkey, cubed
½ cup (125 ml) honey-mustard
  salad dressing

- Combine spinach, walnuts, cranberries, apples and turkey in large salad bowl.

- Toss with salad dressing.

Noodle and Turkey Salad

1 85-g (3-ounce) package
    oriental-flavour ramen
    noodle soup mix
450 g (16 ounces)
    finely shredded
    coleslaw mix
340 g (¾ pound) cooked
    turkey, cut into strips
½ cup (125 ml) vinaigrette salad
    dressing

• Coarsely crush noodles and
  place in bowl with lid. Add
  coleslaw mix and turkey strips.

• Combine vinaigrette salad
  dressing and seasoning packet
  from noodle mix in small bowl.

• Pour over noodle-turkey mixture
  and toss to coat mixture well.
  Refrigerate. Serves 8.

Chicken and Grapefruit Salad

280 g (10 ounces)
    cos lettuce salad mix
600 g (21 ounces)
    grapefruit segments
1 roast chicken,
    boned and cubed
½ red onion, sliced
2 tablespoons (30 ml) orange
    juice
2 tablespoons (30 ml) white wine
    vinegar
2 tablespoons (30 ml) extra-
    virgin olive oil

• Combine salad mix, grapefruit
  sections, chicken and onion in
  salad bowl.

• Combine orange juice, white
  wine, oil plus 1 teaspoon each
  of salt and pepper in small bowl.
  Pour over salad and toss.
  Serves 8.

Bridge Club Luncheon Favourite

1 roast chicken
1 cup (150 g) red grapes, halved
1 cup (150 g) green grapes, halved
2 cups (200 g) chopped celery
⅔ cup (80 g) whole walnuts
⅔ cup (110 g) sliced spring onion
½ cup (110 g) mayonnaise
1 tablespoon (15 ml) orange juice
2 tablespoons (30 ml) red wine vinegar
1 teaspoon chilli powder

- Skin chicken and cut chicken breast into thin strips. (Save dark meat for another meal or use grilled chicken breasts.) Place in bowl with lid.

- Add red and green grapes, celery, walnuts and sliced spring onions.

- Combine mayonnaise, orange juice, vinegar and chilli powder into a bowl, add a little salt and pepper and mix well. Spoon over salad mixture and toss. Refrigerate. Serves 6 to 8.

Wine vinegars are made from red or white wine and derive flavour from the type of wine used.

Herbed Chicken Salad

1 roast chicken
¼ cup (5 g) chopped fresh
  chives
2 tablespoons (20 g) capers
1 cup (100 g) chopped celery
1 cup (245 g) sweet pickles
¼ cup (60 ml) extra-virgin
  olive oil
3 tablespoons (45 ml) white wine
  vinegar
1 teaspoon chopped fresh
  thyme
1 teaspoon oregano
1 tablespoon (15 ml) honey

• Skin chicken and cut meat from bones. Slice chicken into thin strips and place in bowl.

• Add chives, capers, celery and sweet pickles and mix well.

• Whisk olive oil, vinegar, thyme, oregano, honey and a little salt and pepper in bowl. Spoon over chicken salad and toss. Refrigerate. Serves 8.

Fresh chives are in the same family as onions, shallots and garlic. They are high in vitamin C, folic acid and potassium. They have high concentrations of sulphur compounds and essential oils capable of healing properties. Besides the distinctive flavour of chives, they may help the body fight bacteria, ease stomach distress and aid in heart attack and stroke prevention by helping the body digest fat.

Old-Fashioned Chicken or Turkey Salad

3 cups (420 g) cooked, cubed
   chicken or turkey
⅔ cup (70 g) chopped celery
¾ cup (185 g) sweet pickle relish
1 bunch spring onions
   with tops, chopped
3 eggs, hard-boiled and
   chopped
¾ cup (170 g) mayonnaise
Lettuce leaves

- Combine chicken, celery, relish, onions and eggs in bowl.

- Toss with mayonnaise and refrigerate. Serve on lettuce leaves. Serves 6.

Fancy Chicken or Turkey Salad

3 cups (420 g) cooked, cubed
   chicken or turkey
1 cup (100 g) chopped celery
1½ cups (225 g) halved green
   grapes
¾ cup (105 g) cashew nuts
¾ cup (170 g) mayonnaise
1 cup (55 g) chow mein noodles
Cabbage leaves

- Combine chicken, celery, grapes and cashews in bowl, then toss with mayonnaise.

- Just before serving, mix in noodles and serve on cabbage leaves. Serves 6.

Chicken and Rice Salad

3 cups (420 g) cooked, cubed
    chicken or turkey
170 g (6 ounces) long
    grain and wild rice mix,
    cooked and drained
1 bunch spring onions
    with tops, chopped
1 cup (85 g) chopped walnuts
1 230-g (8-ounce) can sliced
    water chestnuts
1 cup (225 g) mayonnaise
¾ teaspoon curry powder
Lettuce

• Combine chicken, rice, spring
  onions, walnuts and water
  chestnuts in bowl. Toss with
  mayonnaise and curry powder
  and refrigerate. Serve on bed
  of lettuce. Serves 8.

Summertime Prawn Salad

1 400-g (14-ounce) package
    frozen tortellini, cooked
450 g (1 pound) cooked, peeled,
    veined prawns
½ cup (65 g) sliced black olives
½ cup (50 g) chopped celery
½ cup (125 ml) zesty Italian salad
    dressing

• Combine pasta, prawns, olives
  and celery in salad bowl.

• Pour salad dressing over salad
  and toss. Serve immediately or
  refrigerate until ready to serve.
  Serves 8.

Wacky Tuna Salad

**1 200-g (7-ounce) tin
cooked, light tuna in water
1 red apple with peel,
cored and chopped
280 g (10 ounces) frozen green
peas, thawed and drained
1 red capsicum, chopped
Shredded lettuce
115 ml (4 ounces) Thousand
Island salad dressing**

½ cup (110 g) mayonnaise

- Place tuna in bowl, add chopped apple, green peas and capsicum and mix well.

- Combine dressing and mayonnaise in bowl, pour over tuna salad and stir to blend well.

- Refrigerate for at least 2 hours and serve over bed of shredded lettuce. Serves 6.

Thaw frozen foods in refrigerator or in the microwave, never at room temperature, which allows unsafe bacterial growth.

Tuna and Tortellini Salad

200 g (7 ounces) tortellini
¼ cup (115 g) butter
1 340-g (12-ounce) can tuna, drained
1 115-g (4-ounce) jar sliced black olives
¾ cup (55 g) pouring cream
1 teaspoon dried basil leaves
2 tablespoons (15 g) parmesan cheese
1 teaspoon salt

- Cook pasta according to package directions and drain. Add butter and stir until butter melts. Add tuna and olives.

- Combine cream, basil, cheese and salt in bowl. Pour over pasta-tuna mixture and toss. Serves 6.

Ribbon or strand pastas *are long, flat pastas of varying length, width and thickness.*

Capelli d'angelo	*'angel hair' pasta; very thin spaghetti*
Fedellini	*very thin spaghetti*
Fettucini	*'little ribbons'; long flat egg pasta strips*
Lasagna	*long wide sheets, usually with rippled edges*
Linguine	*long, narrow strips about ¼ cm wide*
Margherite	*long, narrow strips with one rippled edge*
Spaghetti	*long, thin round strands*
Tagliatelle	*long, flat egg pasta strips about ½ cm wide*
Vermicelli	*very thin spaghetti, similar to angel hair pasta*

Snappy Sandwiches

*Hot, Cold,
Open-Face,
Veggies and Meats*

Snappy Sandwiches Contents

Hot Roast Beef Sandwich

1 340-g (12-ounce) loaf
   French bread
¼ cup (60 g) Dijon-style mustard
340 g (¾ pound) sliced
   roast beef
8 slices cheddar cheese

- Preheat oven to 160° C (325° F).

- Split French bread and spread mustard on bottom slice. Line slices of beef over mustard and cheese slices over beef. Add top of loaf.

- Cut loaf into quarters and place on baking tray. Heat for about 5 minutes or until cheese just partially melts. Serves 4.

Reuben Sandwiches

12 slices dark rye bread
6 slices Swiss cheese
12 thin deli slices
   corned beef
4 cups (500 g) deli coleslaw,
   drained

- On 6 slices of rye bread, layer cheese, 2 slices corned beef and lots of coleslaw. Top with remaining bread slices. Serves 6.

A Different Sandwich

½ cup (110 g) mayonnaise
⅓ cup (85 g) Dijon-style
    mustard
¼ cup (55 g) horseradish
6 18-cm (7-inch) pieces Italian
    focaccia
450 g (1 pound) shaved
    roast beef
1 340-g (12-ounce) jar roasted
    red capsicums, cut
    into strips
6 slices mozzarella cheese
Baby cos lettuce

- Combine mayonnaise, mustard and horseradish into a small bowl. Use serrated knife to slice bread in half horizontally.

- Spread generous amount of dressing on one side of bread.

- Top bread with several slices roast beef, roasted capsicums, cheese, lettuce and remaining bread half.

- To serve, cut sandwiches in half. Serves 6.

Tasty Sub Sandwich

4 15-cm (6-inch) sub rolls
1 onion, halved and thinly
sliced
Olive oil
2 tablespoons (30 g) butter
2 tablespoons (20 g) beef
stock powder
8 slices roast beef
4 slices provolone cheese

- Slice rolls in half lengthwise, place on baking tray and grill until golden brown.

- Preheat oven to 175° C (350° F).

- Cook onion with a little oil in frypan on medium-low heat for 6 minutes. Set aside.

- Heat butter, ½ cup (125 ml) water and beef stock in saucepan. Use tongs to dip beef slices into hot liquid.

- Place beef slices and cheese slices on bottom of 4 rolls. Divide cooked onion over cheese and place tops of rolls over onions.

- Place filled rolls on baking tray and heat for 5 minutes or just until cheese melts. Serves 4.

Most people alternate between the same dozen or so meals for breakfast, lunch and dinner. They usually rotate these and introduce some minor variations throughout most of their lives. Choose your meals wisely.

Southwest Burgers

8 hamburger buns
900 g (2 pounds) lean minced beef
1 30-g (1-ounce) packet taco seasoning mix
1 cup (265 g) salsa
8 slices pepper cheese

- Combine beef, taco seasoning and ¼ cup (65 g) salsa in large bowl. Shape mixture into 8 patties.

- If you are grilling, cook patties for about 12 minutes (or until they cook thoroughly) and turn once.

- To grill in oven, place patties on griller tray 10–13 cm (4–5 inches) from heat and grill until they cook thoroughly. Turn once during cooking.

- When patties are almost done, place buns cut-side down on grill and heat for 1 or 2 minutes.

- Place 8 patties on bottom half of buns, top with cheese and cook for an additional 1 minute or until cheese melts.

- Top with heaped tablespoon of salsa and top half of bun. Serves 8.

Limp vegetables like celery, carrots and even potatoes will regain their crispness and crunch when you soak them in iced water for about 1 hour.

It's a Tortilla Wrap

3 large (30-cm) tortillas
Mayonnaise
1 cup (115 g) shredded cheddar
    cheese
250 g (9 ounces)
    spring salad greens
1 cup (180 g) finely diced,
    drained tomatoes
3 finely chopped spring
    onions
6 slices thin deli turkey
    or ham

- Heat griller, place tortillas on baking tray and grill briefly on each side.

- Remove from oven and spread thin layer of mayonnaise over 1 side of tortillas.

- Sprinkle cheese over tortillas and return to oven just until cheese melts.

- Combine salad greens, tomatoes and spring onions in bowl and sprinkle on tortillas. Place 2 slices of turkey or ham on tortillas. Roll or fold over. Serves 3.

Sprouted grain breads are easier to digest, are more nutritious and maintain freshness longer than other breads. They can be found in the bakery section in the supermarket.

A Family Sandwich

1 230-g (8-ounce) loaf
  French bread
300 ml (10 ounces)
  Dijonnaise
170 g (6 ounces) sliced Swiss
  cheese
170 g (6 ounces) sliced deli ham
8 sliced dill pickles

- Preheat oven to 190° C (375° F).

- Cut bread in half horizontally and spread Dijonnaise over cut sides of bread.

- Arrange half of cheese and half of ham on bottom slice and top with pickle slices. Spread remaining cheese and ham on top of pickles.

- Cover with top of bread, press down on sandwich and cut into quarters. Place on baking tray and bake for 5 minutes. Serve hot. Serves 4.

Open-Face Apple and Ham Sandwiches

Mayonnaise
Mustard
4 round buns
16 slices cheddar cheese
8 thin slices deli ham
1 red delicious apple with peel,
  finely chopped

- Spread a little mayonnaise and mustard on top and bottom of 4 buns and place on baking tray.

- Top each bottom and top with 1 slice of cheese, 1 slice of ham and about 2 tablespoons (15 g) chopped apple. Top with remaining cheese slices.

- Grill 10 to 13 cm (4 to 5 inches) from heat just until top slice of cheese melts. Serve immediately. Serves 8.

Wrap It Up Now!

4 burrito tortillas
¼ cup (60 ml)
   Thousand Island dressing
4 slices deli ham
4 slices Swiss cheese
1½ cups (190 g) deli coleslaw

- Spread tortillas with dressing and place 1 slice ham and 1 slice cheese on each tortilla. Spoon one-quarter of coleslaw on top.

- Roll and wrap each in baking paper. Place in microwave and heat just until cheese melts. Cut wraps in half to serve. Serves 4.

Chicken Sandwich Olé

280 g (10 ounces) frozen,
   crumbed chicken patties
Baguette rolls
½ cup (110 g) spring onion
   dip
⅓ cup (90 g) thick-and-chunky
   hot salsa
Lettuce, shredded
Tomatoes, chopped

- Preheat oven to 160° C (325° F).

- Heat chicken patties in oven according to package directions.

- Place 4 split baguettes in oven for the last 3 minutes of cooking time.

- Spread bottom half of each baguette liberally with dip and salsa. Top each with chicken patty, shredded lettuce and chopped tomatoes.

- Place top baguette over lettuce and tomatoes. Serve immediately. Serves 4.

A Special Toasted Cheese Sandwich

Make as many of these sandwiches as you need. Just multiply the ingredients below.

Butter, softened
1 loaf multigrain bread
Filling for 1 sandwich:
1 tablespoon (15 g) barbecue
   sauce
1 tablespoon (15 g) mayonnaise
2 slices sharp cheddar
   cheese
2 tablespoons (10 g) cooked,
   crumbled bacon
¼ whole avocado,
   thinly sliced

- For each sandwich, spread softened butter on 2 thick slices of multigrain bread. Place 1 slice, butter-side down, in heavy frypan.

- Spread with ½ tablespoon mayonnaise, ½ tablespoon barbecue sauce and 1 slice cheese.

- Sprinkle with crumbled bacon and avocado slices. Top with second slice of cheese and remaining slice of bread spread with ½ tablespoon each of mayonnaise and barbecue sauce.

- Heat frypan on medium-high heat and cook for about 2 minutes or until sandwich is light brown and cheese is melted.

- Turn sandwich over and cook for an additional 2 minutes or until cheese melts completely. Serves 2.

Sunday Night Chicken Sandwiches

280 g (10 ounces) frozen, crumbed chicken breast patties
Olive oil
170 g (6 ounces) guacamole dip
⅓ cup (90 g) thick-and-chunky salsa
130 g (4½ ounces) shredded lettuce
4 wholemeal hamburger buns, split

- Cook chicken breast patties according to package directions in frypan with very little oil.

- Spread thin layer of guacamole dip on bottom of each bun, top each with chicken patty and spread salsa on top of patty.

- Place 3 to 4 tablespoons (15 to 20 g) shredded lettuce over salsa. Spread another thin layer of guacamole on top bun and place over each filled bottom bun. Serves 4.

Olive oil originated in Asia, but has been cultivated in the Mediterranean for thousands of years. One tablespoon of olive oil has 550 kilojoules and 14 grams of fat, mostly monounsaturated fat that has a positive effect on cholesterol levels. It is also used for dry skin, as prevention for hair loss and for earaches.

Italian-Sausage Sandwiches

**450 g (1 pound) sweet Italian
    sausages**
1 red capsicum, chopped
1 onion, chopped
**1⅔ cups (410 g) Italian-style
    spaghetti sauce**
Baguette rolls

- Remove casing from sausages
  and cook with capsicum and
  onion in frypan over medium
  heat until sausage browns.

- Stir in spaghetti sauce and heat
  until boiling. Simmer for
  5 minutes and stir constantly.
  Pour mixture over split
  baguettes. Serves 4 to 6.

Confetti Sandwiches

1 tablespoon (15 ml) lemon juice
**225 g (8 ounces) cream
    cheese, softened**
Mayonnaise
½ cup (55 g) grated carrots
¼ cup (30 g) grated cucumber
**¼ cup (40 g) grated purple
    onion**
¼ cup (35 g) grated capsicum

- Combine lemon juice with
  cream cheese and add enough
  mayonnaise to make cheese into
  a spreading consistency.

- Fold in grated vegetables, spread
  on bread for sandwiches and
  refrigerate. Serves 4.

'Honey' Open-Face Sandwich

⅓ cup (85 ml) honey-mustard dressing
4 round rolls, split
8 thin slices deli honey ham
8 slices Swiss cheese

- Preheat oven to 205° C (400° F).

- Spread honey-mustard dressing on each split roll. Top each with ham and cheese slices.

- Place on baking tray and bake for 4 to 5 minutes or until cheese melts. Serves 4.

Pizza Sandwich

6 English muffins
450 g (1 pound) sausages, cooked and drained
1½ cups (375 ml) pizza sauce
1 115-g (4-ounce) can mushrooms, drained
230 g (8 ounces) shredded mozzarella cheese

- Split muffins and layer ingredients on each muffin half, ending with cheese.

- Grill until cheese melts. Serves 6.

You can buy sausages in several forms: fresh, cured, cooked, uncooked or dried. Read the labels carefully for cooking instructions.

Meatball Heroes

450 g (16 ounces)
   tomato-based pasta sauce
450 g (16 ounces) frozen
   capsicum, thawed
½ onion, minced
340 g (12 ounces) frozen
   meatballs, thawed
French rolls*

- Combine pasta sauce, capsicum
  and onion in large saucepan and
  cook on medium heat for
  5 minutes.

- Add meatballs, cover and gently
  boil for about 5 minutes or until
  meatballs are hot.

- Spoon into split French rolls and
  serve hot. Serves 8.

*TIP: Any bread, such as club
   rolls, hot dog buns or French
   rolls, will work.

Provolone and Capsicum Burgers

⅓ cup (45 g) finely cubed
   provolone cheese
¼ cup (50 g) diced roasted red
   capsicums
¼ cup (40 g) finely chopped
   onion
450 g (1 pound) lean minced beef
4 hamburger buns, split

- Combine cheese, red capsicum,
  onion and a little salt and pepper
  in bowl. Add beef, mix well and
  shape into 4 patties.

- Grill patties over medium-hot
  heat for 5 minutes on each side
  or until meat is no longer pink.

- Add your favourite lettuce,
  tomatoes, etc., and serve on
  hamburger buns. Serves 4.

Turkey and Asparagus Sandwiches

4 slices cheddar cheese
2 English muffins,
    split and toasted
230 g (½ pound) thinly sliced
    turkey
1 425-g (15-ounce) can
    asparagus spears,
    drained
50–100 ml (1½–3½ ounces)
    hollandaise sauce
Paprika (optional)

- Place 1 cheese slice on each muffin half and top evenly with turkey.

- Cut asparagus spears to fit muffin halves and top each with 3 or 4 asparagus spears. (Reserve remaining asparagus for another use.)

- Pour hollandaise sauce evenly over sandwiches and sprinkle with paprika, if desired. Serves 4.

Fruited Chicken Salad

280 g (10 ounces)
    spring salad greens
170 g (6 ounces) cooked
    chicken strips
½ cup (90 g) fresh strawberries
½ cup (60 g) fresh raspberries
½ fresh peach, sliced
230 g (8 ounces) raspberry salad
    dressing
Lettuce
Crackers or breadsticks

- Combine salad greens, chicken strips, berries and peach in salad bowl.

- Toss with just enough salad dressing to coat salad. Put on multigrain bread or serve on a bed of lettuce with bread, crackers or breadsticks. Serves 4.

Wrap-That-Turkey Burger

450 g (1 pound) minced turkey
⅓ cup (40 g) shredded cheese
¼ cup (40 g) finely grated
**   onion**
1 teaspoon Cajun seasoning
4 fajita tortillas, warmed
2 cups (70 g) shredded lettuce
⅔ cup (150 g) prepared
**   guacamole**

- Combine turkey, cheese, onion and seasoning in bowl.

- Shape into 4 patties (make patties a little longer than round) and refrigerate about 30 minutes before cooking.

- Grill patties about 13 cm (5 inches) from heat for about 8 minutes or until a meat thermometer inserted in the patty reads 70° C (165° F).

- Place tortillas on flat surface and arrange one-quarter lettuce on each tortilla. Place 1 patty on each tortilla and spread with guacamole. Fold tortilla in half to cover filling. Serves 4.

TIP: If you don't want to buy
*   Cajun seasoning, use*
*   1 teaspoon salt and*
*   ¼ teaspoon cayenne pepper.*

BLT Tortilla Wraps

2 flour tortillas
Mayonnaise, to taste
2 slices turkey
2 slices cooked bacon
Shredded lettuce, to taste
1 medium tomato, chopped

- Spread each tortilla with mayonnaise. Add 2 slices turkey, 2 slices bacon and shredded lettuce and tomato.

- Fold edges over to enclose filling. Serve immediately or wrap in baking paper and refrigerate. Makes 2.

TIP: This recipe is great for lunch with friends, just multiply the ingredients.

Walnut-Cream Sandwiches

450 g (16 ounces) cream
    cheese, softened
½ cup (110 g) mayonnaise
1 teaspoon Dijon-style
    mustard
6 slices bacon,
    cooked and crumbled
¾ cup (65 g) finely chopped
    walnuts
Pumpernickel or rye
    bread

- Beat cream cheese, mayonnaise and mustard in bowl until creamy. Fold in bacon and walnuts and mix well.

- Spread on pumpernickel or rye bread and slice in thirds. Serves 6.

Crab and Avocado Burgers

4 frozen crab cakes
1 ripe avocado
¼ cup (55 g) mayonnaise
1 tablespoon (15 ml) lemon juice
1 115-g (4-ounce) can green
    chillies, drained
4 hamburger buns
Lettuce
Tomatoes

- Microwave crab cakes according to package directions. Mash avocado, mayonnaise, lemon juice and ½ teaspoon salt in bowl with fork. Stir in green chillies.

- Place crab cakes on buns and spread with avocado-mayonnaise mixture. Serve as is or top with lettuce and sliced tomatoes. Serves 4.

Hot Bunwiches

8 hamburger buns
8 slices Swiss cheese
8 slices deli ham
8 slices deli turkey
8 slices cheddar cheese

- Lay out all 8 buns and place slices of Swiss cheese, ham, turkey and cheddar cheese on bottom buns.

- Place top bun over cheddar cheese, wrap each bunwich individually in foil and place in freezer. Remove from freezer 2 to 3 hours before serving.

- When ready to heat, preheat oven to 160° C (325° F).

- Heat for about 30 minutes and serve hot. Serves 8.

Seafood Tortilla Wraps

2 23-cm (9-inch) tortillas
Mayonnaise, to taste
1 cup (115 g) shredded cheddar
    cheese
250 g (9 ounces) spring salad
    greens
1 cup (255 g) diced tomatoes,
    drained
4 spring onions, finely
    chopped
1 115-g (4-ounce) can
    tuna fillets with lemon and
    cracked pepper, crumbled

- Heat griller, place tortillas on baking tray and grill very briefly on each side.

- Remove from oven and spread mayonnaise on 1 side of tortilla.

- Spread cheese over tortillas and return to oven just until cheese melts.

- Combine salad greens, tomatoes and spring onions in bowl and sprinkle on tortillas.

- Place as much of crumbled tuna on tortilla as needed.

- Roll or fold over to eat.
  Serves 2.

A tortilla is a flat bread made from corn or wheat flour.

Salmon Burgers

1 425-g (15-ounce) can salmon
   with liquid
1 egg, slightly beaten
2 tablespoons (30 ml) lemon juice
⅔ cup (80 g) seasoned
   breadcrumbs
Hamburger buns
Mayonnaise
Lettuce
Sliced tomatoes

- Combine salmon with
  2 tablespoons (30 ml) liquid
  from salmon can, egg, lemon
  juice, breadcrumbs and a little
  salt and pepper in bowl.

- Form into patties and fry with
  a little oil in frypan both sides
  until golden. Serve hot on buns
  with mayonnaise, lettuce and
  sliced tomatoes. Serve 6.

Fish and Chips Sandwiches

1 340-g (12-ounce) box frozen
   crumbed fish fillets,
   thawed
4 Turkish bread rolls
1 cup (125 g) deli coleslaw
30 g (4 ounces) potato chips

- Heat fish fillets according to
  package directions. Remove
  from oven and preheat griller.
  Slice Turkish breads in half
  lengthwise and grill, cut-side up.

- Layer coleslaw, fish fillets
  and potato chips on bread and
  cover with bread tops. Serve
  immediately. Serve 4.

Savoury
Soups & Stews

Cheeses, Beans,
Veggies, Greens
and Meats

Savoury Soups & Stews Contents

*It is best to check your seasonings after cooking.
Sometimes the flavours may cook out over long periods
of time and you may need to add some seasonings again.*

The Ultimate Cheddar Cheese Soup

1 cup (160 g) finely chopped
    onion
1 red capsicum, diced
2 tablespoons (30 g) butter
450 g (16 ounces) shredded
    extra sharp cheddar cheese
2 tablespoons (20 g) cornflour
400 ml (14 ounces) chicken
    stock
1½ cups (210 g) cooked, diced
    ham
1½ cups (105 g) cooked broccoli
    florets
¾ cup (95 g) cooked, diced
    carrots
1 teaspoon
    Worcestershire sauce
½ teaspoon garlic powder
500 ml (1 pint)
    unthickened cream

- Sauté onion and capsicum in butter in large saucepan. Mix cheese and cornflour in bowl. Pour stock into saucepan and add cheese-cornflour mixture a little at a time.

- Cook soup over medium heat until cheese melts. Stir until smooth and creamy.

- Add ham, broccoli, carrots, Worcestershire sauce, garlic powder and a little salt and pepper and stir well. Heat over low heat, pour in cream and stir well. Serves 6 to 8.

Easy Spinach Soup

560 g (20 ounces) frozen chopped spinach, cooked
2 280-g (10-ounce) cans cream of mushroom soup
1 cup (250 ml) unthickened cream
400 ml (14 ounces) chicken stock

- Place spinach, mushroom soup and cream in blender and puree until smooth.

- Place spinach mixture and chicken stock in saucepan and heat on medium heat until hot.

- Reduce heat to low and simmer for 20 minutes. Serve hot or cold. Serve 6.

Speedy Creamy Broccoli and Rice Soup

1 170-g (6-ounce) package chicken-flavoured instant rice mix
280 g (10 ounces) chopped broccoli florets
2 280-g (10-ounce) cans cream of chicken soup
340 g (12 ounces) chicken breast, cooked and chopped

- Combine rice mix, seasoning packet and 5 cups (1.2 L) water in soup pot. Bring to a boil, reduce heat and simmer for 15 minutes.

- Stir in broccoli, chicken soup and chicken. Cover and simmer for additional 5 minutes. Serves 6.

Mexican-Style Minestrone Soup

230 g (8 ounces) mixed
frozen vegetables
200 g (7 ounces) spiral
pasta, cooked
1 teaspoon garlic powder
450 g (16 ounces) thick-
and-chunky salsa
1 425-g (15-ounce) can borlotti
beans with liquid
1 teaspoon chilli powder
1 teaspoon cumin
230 g (8 ounces) shredded
cheddar cheese
1 teaspoon Mexican seasoning

- Combine vegetables, pasta, garlic powder, salsa, borlotti beans, chilli powder, cumin and 1 cup (250 ml) water in large saucepan.

- Heat to boiling, reduce heat to medium-low and simmer for about 8 minutes, stirring occasionally or until vegetables are tender. When ready to serve, top each serving with mixed cheeses and Mexican seasoning. Serves 6.

Fiesta Soup

1 425-g (15-ounce) can
tomatoes
1 425-g (15-ounce) can corn
1 425-g (15-ounce) can borlotti
beans
400 ml (14 ounces) chicken
stock
1 280-g (10-ounce) can
spicy tomato soup
½ cup cheddar cheese spread
2 teaspoons Mexican seasoning

- Combine tomatoes, corn, borlotti beans, chicken stock and a little salt in soup pot on high heat and mix well.

- Stir in tomato soup, cheese and seasoning, and heat just until thoroughly hot. If you feel the soup needs a touch of meat, just add 340 g (12 ounces) cooked white chicken chunks. Serves 6.

Borlotti Bean Soup

800 ml (28 ounces) chicken stock
3 425-g (15-ounce) cans
    borlotti beans, rinsed
    and drained
2 280-g (10-ounce) cans
    tomatoes
100 g (3½ ounces) green chillies,
    sliced
1 onion, chopped
1 teaspoon ground cumin
½ teaspoon dried thyme
½ teaspoon dried oregano
2–3 cups (280–420 g) cooked,
    finely diced ham

- Combine chicken stock and beans in slow cooker and turn cooker to high. Cook just long enough for ingredients to get hot.

- With potato masher, mash about half of beans in slow cooker. Reduce heat to low and add tomatoes, green chillies, onion, spices, ham and ¾ cup (175 ml) water.

- Cover and cook for 5 to 6 hours. Serves 4 to 6.

Fresh chopped parsley added in the last few minutes of cooking adds a wonderful fresh flavour to soups and stews.

Cannellini Bean Soup

8 slices thick-cut bacon,
   divided
1 carrot
3 425-g (15-ounce) cans
   cannellini beans with
   liquid
3 sticks celery, chopped
1 onion, chopped
800 ml (27 ounces)
   chicken stock
1 teaspoon Italian
   herb seasoning
1 280-g (10-ounce) can
   cream of chicken
   soup

- Cook bacon in frypan, drain and crumble. Reserve 2 crumbled slices for garnish. Cut carrot in half lengthwise and slice.

- Combine crumbled bacon, carrot, beans, celery, onion, stock, seasoning and 1 cup (250 ml) water in 5 to 6-L (5 to 6-quart) slow cooker and stir to mix.

- Cover and cook on low for 5 to 6 hours. Ladle 2 cups (500 ml) soup mixture into food processor or blender and process until smooth.

- Return to cooker, add cream of chicken soup and stir to mix. Turn heat to high and cook for additional 10 to 15 minutes. Serves 4 to 6.

Easy Meaty Minestrone

2 560-g (20-ounce) cans minestrone soup
1 425-g (15-ounce) can borlotti beans with juice
1 510-g (18-ounce) package frozen meatballs, thawed
145 g (5 ounces) grated parmesan cheese

- Combine soup, beans, meatballs and ½ cup (125 ml) water in large saucepan.

- Bring to a boil, reduce heat to low and simmer for about 15 minutes. To serve, sprinkle each serving with parmesan cheese. Serves 6 to 8.

Mexican Bean Soup

2 onions, finely chopped
Canola oil
3 teaspoons minced garlic
3 teaspoons chilli powder
3 425-g (15-ounce) cans kidney beans
1 teaspoon cumin
400 ml (14 ounces) beef stock
Shredded cheese or salsa

- Sauté onions in soup pot with a little oil and cook on medium heat for 5 minutes. Stir in garlic and chilli powder.

- Puree 1 can beans and add to onion mixture. Add remaining beans, cumin and beef stock.

- Bring to a boil, reduce heat and simmer for 10 minutes. When serving, garnish with shredded cheese or salsa. Serves 4.

Southern Greens Stew

**900 g (2 pounds) frozen
chopped spinach
200 g (7 ounces) frozen
diced capsicum
½ brown onion, diced
2 cups (280 g) cooked,
chopped ham
1 teaspoon sugar
800 ml (27 ounces)
chicken stock**

- Combine spinach, onions, capsicum, ham, sugar, chicken stock and 1 teaspoon (5 ml) black pepper in soup pot.

- Boil mixture, reduce heat, cover and simmer for 30 minutes. Serves 6.

Potato Talk Soup

**5 medium potatoes,
peeled and cubed
2 cups (280 g) cooked, cubed
ham
1 cup (70 g) fresh broccoli
florets, cut very, very fine
400 g (14 ounces) processed
cheese spread
100 g (3½ ounces) chilli salsa
400 ml (14 ounces) chicken
stock
2½ soup cans (625 ml) milk
Paprika**

- Place potatoes, ham and broccoli in sprayed slow cooker.

- Combine cheese, salsa, stock and milk in saucepan. Heat just enough to mix until smooth. Stir into slow cooker. Cover and cook on low for 7 to 9 hours.

- When serving, sprinkle a little paprika over each serving, if desired. Serves 6.

Split-Pea Soup

1½ cups (300 g) dry yellow
    split peas
2–3 cups (280–420 g) cooked,
    diced ham
1 425-g (15-ounce) can corn
1 280-g (10-ounce) package
    frozen, sliced okra,
    thawed
1 onion, chopped
1 large potato, cubed
2 teaspoons Cajun
    seasoning
400 ml (14 ounces)
    chicken stock
2 425-g (15-ounce) cans
    tomatoes
1 teaspoon Mexican seasoning

- Rinse split peas and drain.
  Combine peas and 5 cups (1.2 L)
  water in large saucepan. Bring to
  a boil, reduce heat, simmer for
  about 10 minutes and drain.

- Combine peas, ham, corn,
  okra, onion, potato, Cajun
  seasoning, stock and 2 cups
  (500 ml) water in 5 to 6-L
  (5 to 6-quart) slow cooker.

- Cover and cook on low for 6 to
  8 hours. Add tomatoes and Mexican
  seasoning and continue cooking
  for additional 1 hour. Serves 6.

*To make a good base for your soup, you can use
any of the following: canned soups (such as cream
of mushroom soup), canned tomatoes, tomato juice,
commercial chicken stock, homemade stocks, commercial soup
bases, seafood stock or bacon for extra flavour.*

Corn and Ham Chowder

400 ml (14 ounces)
  chicken stock
1 cup (250 ml) milk
1 280-g (10-ounce) can cream
  of celery soup
1 425-g (15-ounce) can
  creamed corn
1 425-g (15-ounce) can corn
½ cup (30 g) dry potato
  flakes
1 onion, chopped
2–3 cups (280–420 g) cooked,
  chopped, ham

• Combine stock, milk, soup,
  creamed corn, corn kernels,
  potato flakes, onion and ham in
  6-L (6-quart) slow cooker.

• Cover and cook on low for 4 to
  5 hours. When ready to serve,
  season with a little salt and
  black pepper. Serves 6.

Easy Pork Tenderloin Stew

*This is a great recipe for
leftover pork or beef.*

2–3 cups (280–420 g) cooked,
  cubed pork
340 g (12 ounces) pork gravy
¼ cup (70 g) chilli sauce
450 g (16 ounces) frozen
  stew vegetables
Mashed potato or rice

• Combine pork, gravy, chilli
  sauce, stew vegetables and
  ½ cup (125 ml) water in
  soup pot.

• Bring to a boil and boil for 2
  minutes; reduce heat and simmer
  for 10 minutes. Serve with
  mashed potato or rice. Serves 4.

Ham and Vegetable Chowder

This is a great recipe for leftover ham.

1 medium potato
2 280-g (10-ounce) cans cream
    of celery soup
400 ml (14 ounces) chicken stock
2 cups (280 g) cooked, finely
    diced ham
1 425-g (15-ounce) can corn
2 carrots, sliced

1 onion, coarsely chopped
1 teaspoon dried basil
280 g (10 ounces) frozen broccoli
    florets

- Cut potato into 2-cm (1-inch) pieces. Combine all ingredients except broccoli in large slow cooker.

- Cover and cook on low for 5 to 6 hours. Add broccoli and about ½ teaspoon each of salt and pepper to cooker and cook for additional 1 hour. Serves 4.

The word chowder comes from the French word 'chaudiere', a cauldron in which fishermen made their stews fresh from the sea. Chowder is a thick soup containing chunky food, often seafood.

Easy Potato Soup

**500 g (18 ounces) frozen
 hash browns shredded
1 cup (160 g) chopped onion
400 ml (14 ounces) chicken
 stock
1 280-g (10-ounce) can cream
 of celery soup
1 280-g (10-ounce) can cream
 of chicken soup
2 cups (500 ml) milk**

- Combine hash browns, onion
 and 2 cups (500 ml) water in
 large saucepan and bring to a
 boil.

- Cover, reduce heat and simmer
 for 30 minutes.

- Stir in stock, soups and milk and
 heat thoroughly. (If you like,
 garnish with shredded cheddar
 cheese or cooked, diced ham.)
 Serves 6.

Potato and Sausage Soup

**450 g (1 pound) pork sausages
1 cup (100 g) chopped celery
1 cup (160 g) chopped onion
2 280-g (10-ounce) cans
 potato soup
800 ml (28 ounces)
 chicken stock**

- Cut sausages into 2-cm
 (1-inch) slices.

- Brown sausage slices in large
 heavy frypan, then remove
 sausage to separate bowl.

- Leave about 2 tablespoons
 (30 ml) sausage drippings
 in frypan and sauté celery
 and onion.

- Add potato soup, ¾ cup
 (175 ml) water, chicken stock
 and cooked sausage slices.
 Bring to a boil, reduce heat
 and simmer for 20 minutes.
 Serves 6.

Chickpea Stew

1 450-g (16-ounce) pork and beef salami ring, thinly sliced
2 onions, chopped
3 sticks celery, chopped
Canola oil
3 425-g (15-ounce) cans chickpeas, drained and rinsed
2 280-g (10-ounce) cans diced tomatoes
60 g (2 ounces) green chillies, sliced
800 ml (27 ounces) chicken stock

- Place salami slices, onion and celery in soup pot with a little oil and cook until sausage is slightly brown and onion is soft. Drain and discard fat.

- Add beans, tomatoes, green chillies and stock. Bring mixture to a boil, reduce heat and simmer for 30 minutes.

- Take out about 2 to 3 cups (500 to 750 ml) soup mixture, place in blender and pulse until almost smooth. Return mixture to soup pot and stir to thicken stew.

- Return heat to high until stew is thoroughly hot. Serves 6.

Need to thicken your soup? Adding a little pasta or mashed potato flakes is a great way to add body to your soup.

Polish Vegetable Stew

Canola oil
1 onion, sliced
1 carrot, sliced
2 425-g (15-ounce) cans
   tomatoes
450 g (1 pound) Polish
   sausage
2 425-g (15-ounce) cans
   new potatoes, quartered
250 g (9 ounces) coleslaw mix

- Place a little oil in large soup pot. Cook onion and carrot slices for 3 minutes or until tender but crisp and add tomatoes.

- Cut sausage into 2-cm (1-inch) pieces. Add potatoes and sausage to soup mixture.

- Bring to a boil, reduce heat and simmer for 10 minutes.

- Stir in coleslaw mix, cook for additional 8 minutes and stir occasionally. Serves 6.

Italian Chickpea Soup

450 g (16 ounces) frozen
   diced capsicums
1 brown onion, diced
Canola oil
450 g (1 pound) Italian
   sausages, sliced
400 ml (14 ounces) beef
   stock
1 425-g (15-ounce) can
   Italian tomatoes
2 425-g (15-ounce) cans
   chickpeas, rinsed and
   drained

- Sauté onions and capsicums in soup pot with a little oil. Add Italian sausages and cook until brown. Stir in beef stock, tomatoes and chickpeas.

- Bring mixture to a boil, reduce heat and simmer for about 30 minutes. Serves 6.

Quick Spicy Tomato Soup

**2 280-g (10-ounce) cans
     tomato soup**
**1 425-g (15-ounce) can
     tomatoes**
1 teaspoon Mexican seasoning
Sour cream
**230 g (½ pound) bacon,
     fried, drained and
     crumbled**

- Combine soup, tomatoes and seasoning in saucepan and heat.

- To serve, place dollop of sour cream on top of soup and sprinkle crumbled bacon over sour cream. Serves 4.

Spaghetti Soup

200 g (7 ounces) spaghetti
**1 500-g (18-ounce) package
     frozen, cooked
     meatballs, thawed**
**1 795-g (28-ounce) jar spaghetti
     sauce**
1 425-g (15-ounce) can tomatoes

- Cook pasta in soup pot with 3 L (3 quarts) boiling water and a little salt for about 6–8 minutes (no need to drain).

- When pasta is done, add meatballs, spaghetti sauce and tomatoes and cook until mixture heats through. Serves 6.

TIP: To garnish each soup bowl, sprinkle with 2 tablespoons (15 g) mozzarella cheese or whatever cheese you have in the refrigerator.

Spicy Sausage Soup

1 kg (2 pounds) sausage meat
2 teaspoons chilli flakes
2 425-g (15-ounce) cans
  tomatoes
3 cups (300 g) chopped
  celery
1 cup (120 g) sliced carrots
1 425-g (15-ounce) can sliced
  green beans, drained
400 ml (14 ounces)
  chicken stock
1 teaspoon sweet paprika
1 teaspoon Cajun seasoning

- Shape sausage meat into small balls and place in non-stick frypan.

- Brown thoroughly and drain. Place in large slow cooker.

- Add remaining ingredients plus 2 teaspoons salt and 1 cup (250 ml) water. Stir gently so meatballs will not break up.

- Cover and cook on low for 6 to 7 hours. Serves 6.

If your sauce, soup or stew is too salty, add a peeled potato to the pot and it will absorb the extra salt. You can also add some potato flakes if you have them.

Enchilada Soup

450 g (1 pound) lean minced beef, browned and drained
1 425-g (15-ounce) can tomatoes
1 425-g (15-ounce) can borlotti beans with liquid
1 425-g (15-ounce) can corn with liquid
1 onion, chopped
560 g (20 ounces) enchilada sauce
100 g (3½ ounces) shredded parmesan cheese
130 g (4½ ounces) shredded cheddar cheese
Corn chips, crushed (optional)

- Combine beef, tomatoes, beans, corn, onion, enchilada sauce and 1 cup (250 ml) water in sprayed 5 to 6-L (5 to 6-quart) slow cooker and mix well.

- Cover and cook on low for 6 to 8 hours or on high for 3 to 4 hours.

- Stir in shredded cheese. If desired, top each serving with a few crushed corn chips. Serves 6.

Did you know ice cubes love fat? If you drop a few cubes into your soup, fat will cling to them and it's easy to remove it.

Mexican Meatball Soup

1.2 L (2½ pints) beef stock
450 g (16 ounces) hot salsa
450 g (16 ounces) frozen
    corn, thawed
1 455-g (16-ounce) package
    frozen meatballs,
    thawed
1 teaspoon minced
    garlic

- Combine all ingredients in slow cooker and stir well.

- Cover and cook on low for 4 to 7 hours. Serves 6.

Beefy Vegetable Soup

450 g (1 pound) lean minced
    beef
1.4 L (46 ounces) cocktail
    vegetable juice
1 30-g (1-ounce) packet onion
    soup mix
1 85-g (3-ounce) package
    beef-flavoured
    ramen noodles
450 g (16 ounces) frozen
    mixed vegetables

- Brown beef in large soup pot over medium heat and drain. Stir in vegetable juice, soup mix, contents of noodle seasoning packet and mixed vegetables.

- Heat mixture to boiling, reduce heat and simmer for 6 minutes or until vegetables are tender but crisp. Return to boiling, stir in noodles and cook for 3 minutes. Serves 6.

Hamburger Soup

900 g (2 pounds) lean
  minced beef
2 425-g (15-ounce) cans
  chilli
450 g (16 ounces) frozen mixed
  vegetables, thawed
1.2 L (2½ pints) beef stock
2 425-g (15-ounce) cans
  tomatoes

- Brown beef in frypan and place in 6-L (6-quart) slow cooker.

- Add chilli, vegetables, stock, tomatoes, 1 cup (250 ml) water and 1 teaspoon salt and stir well. Cover and cook on low for 6 to 7 hours. Serves 6.

Taco Soup

680 g (1½ pounds) lean
  minced beef
1 30-g (1-ounce) packet
  taco seasoning
2 425-g (15-ounce) cans
  tomatoes
2 425-g (15-ounce) cans
  chilli beans with
  liquid
1 425-g (15-ounce) can corn,
  drained
Corn chips, crushed
Shredded cheddar cheese

- Brown beef in frypan and place in 5 to 6-L (5 to 6-quart) slow cooker. Add taco seasoning, tomatoes, chilli beans, corn and 1 cup (250 ml) water and mix well.

- Cover and cook on low for 4 hours or on high for 1 to 2 hours. Serve over crushed corn chips and sprinkle some shredded cheddar cheese over top of each serving. Serves 6.

Taco Soup Olé

**900 g (2 pounds) lean
   minced beef**
**2 425-g (15-ounce) cans kidney
   beans with liquid**
**1 425-g (15-ounce) can
   corn, drained**
**2 425-g (15-ounce) cans
   tomatoes**
**100 g (3½ ounces) green chillies,
   sliced**
**60 ml (2 ounces) ranch
   dressing**
**2 30-g (1-ounce) packets
   taco seasoning**

- Brown beef in large frypan, drain and transfer to slow cooker.

- Add remaining ingredients and stir well. Cover and cook on low for 8 to 10 hours. Serves 6.

TIP: For a nice touch, sprinkle shredded cheddar cheese over each serving.

A real time-saver is to make a large pot of soup or stew and divide it into serving portions in resealable plastic bags. Freeze enough for one, two or four. When the bag is sealed, it will lie flat in the freezer and won't take up as much room as containers. Be sure to leave a little room for expansion as it freezes.

Meatball Stew I

**500 g (18 ounces) frozen
 meatballs, thawed**
**400 ml (14 ounces)
 beef stock**
**2 425-g (15-ounce) cans
 Italian tomatoes**
**450 g (16 ounces) frozen stew
 vegetables**

- Place meatballs, beef stock and
  tomatoes in large saucepan.
  Bring to boiling, reduce heat and
  simmer for 10 minutes or until
  meatballs are thoroughly hot.

- Add vegetables and cook on
  medium heat for 10 minutes.
  Mixture will be fairly thin.
  Serves 6.

*TIP: If you like thicker stew, thicken
     this by mixing 2 tablespoons
     (15 g) cornflour in ¼ cup
     (60 ml) water and stir into
     stew. Bring to boiling and stir
     constantly until stew thickens.*

Meatball Stew II

**500 g (18 ounces) frozen
 meatballs, thawed**
500 ml (14 ounces) beef stock
**1 425-g (15-ounce) can
 green beans**
**450 g (16 ounces) baby
 carrots**
**2 425-g (15-ounce) cans
 tomatoes**
**1 tablespoon (15 ml)
 Worcestershire sauce**
**½ teaspoon ground
 allspice**

- Combine all ingredients in slow
  cooker. Cover and cook on low
  for 3 to 5 hours. Serves 6.

Quick Brunswick Stew

This is great with fresh bread!

**2 425-g (15-ounce) cans
beef stew
1 425-g (15-ounce) can butter
beans with liquid
2 425-g (15-ounce) cans
tomatoes with liquid
1 425-g (15-ounce) can
corn, drained
½ teaspoon Tabasco
sauce (optional)**

• Combine beef stew, beans, tomatoes and corn in large stew pot. Bring stew to a boil on medium-high heat, reduce heat and simmer for 35 minutes. Serves 6.

TIP: Brunswick stew needs to be a little spicy, so stir in Tabasco sauce. If you don't want the 'spicy', add 1 tablespoon (15 ml) Worcestershire sauce to the stew.

When you're pouring soup or stew from one container to another, pour it over the back of a large spoon. The spoon will reduce the splatter and the process will have less clean-up.

Chicken and Pasta Soup

680 g (1½ pounds) boneless, skinless chicken thighs, cubed
1 onion, chopped
3 carrots, sliced
½ cup (65 g) halved, pitted black olives
1 teaspoon minced garlic
1.2 L (2½ pints) chicken stock
1 425-g (15-ounce) can Italian tomatoes
1 teaspoon Italian seasoning
½ cup (40 g) small shell pasta
Parmesan cheese

- Combine all ingredients except pasta and parmesan cheese in slow cooker.

- Cover and cook on low for 8 to 9 hours. About 30 minutes before serving, add pasta and stir.

- Increase heat to high and cook for additional 20 to 30 minutes. Serve with parmesan cheese. Serves 6.

If you cook your pasta before adding it to your soup, it doesn't bring all the starch with it and can be added last so it doesn't get overcooked. You can even use leftover pasta that you have in the refrigerator.

White Lightning Chilli

3 425-g (15-ounce) cans
    cannellini beans with
    liquid
1.2 L (2½ pints) chicken
    stock
1 280-g (10-ounce) can cream
    of chicken soup
2 tablespoons (30 g) butter,
    melted
2 onions, chopped
3 cups (420 g) cooked,
    chopped chicken
    or turkey
1 200-g (7-ounce) jar chopped
    green chillies
1 teaspoon minced garlic

½ teaspoon dried basil
½ teaspoon white pepper
⅛ teaspoon cayenne
    pepper
⅛ teaspoon ground cloves
1 teaspoon ground
    oregano
230 g (8 ounces) shredded
    cheddar blend

- Combine all ingredients
  except cheese in slow cooker.
  Cover and cook on low for
  4 to 5 hours.

- When serving, sprinkle cheese
  over top of each serving.
  Serves 6.

Country Chicken Chowder

680 g (1½ pounds) boneless, skinless chicken breast halves
2 tablespoons (30 g) butter
2 280-g (10-ounce) cans potato and leek soup
400 ml (14 ounces) chicken stock
230 g (8 ounces) frozen corn
1 onion, sliced
2 sticks celery, sliced
1 280-g (10-ounce) package frozen peas and carrots, thawed
½ teaspoon dried thyme leaves
½ cup (125 ml) unthickened cream

- Cut chicken into 2-cm (1-inch) strips.

- Brown chicken strips in butter in frypan and transfer to large slow cooker.

- Add soup, stock, corn, onion, celery, peas, carrots and thyme and stir.

- Cover and cook on low for 3 to 4 hours or until vegetables are tender. Turn off heat, stir in cream and set aside for about 10 minutes before serving. Serves 6.

Confetti Chicken Soup

450 g (1 pound) skinless, boneless chicken thighs

1 170-g (6-ounce) package chicken-flavoured rice

1.2 L (2½ pints) chicken stock

3 carrots, sliced

1 280-g (10-ounce) can cream of chicken soup

1½ tablespoons (20 g) chicken seasoning

280 g (10 ounces) frozen corn, thawed

280 g (10 ounces) frozen baby green peas, thawed

- Cut thighs into thin strips. Combine chicken, rice, stock, carrots, soup, seasoning and 1 cup (250 ml) water in 5 to 6-L (5 to 6-quart) slow cooker.

- Cover and cook on low for 8 to 9 hours.

- About 30 minutes before serving, turn heat to high and add corn and peas to cooker. Continue cooking for additional 30 minutes. Serves 6.

Use frozen vegetables such as peas, spinach or corn to cut prep time when making soup. Add them to assorted soups or puree them with stock, cream and sautéed onion and simmer to make a smooth soup.

Tasty Turkey Soup

340 g (12 ounces) frozen
    chopped capsicum
100 g (3½ ounces) onion, diced
Canola oil
2 85-g (3-ounce) packages
    chicken-flavoured
    ramen noodles
2 280-g (10-ounce) cans
    cream of chicken
    soup
1 cup (140 g) leftover cubed
    turkey

- Cook capsicum and onions in soup pot with a little oil just until tender but not brown. Add ramen noodles, seasoning packet and 2 cups (500 ml) water. Cook for 5 minutes or until noodles are tender.

- Stir in chicken soup and turkey. Heat, stirring constantly until thoroughly hot. Serves 6.

So Easy Peanut Soup

2 280-g (10-ounce) cans
    cream of chicken
    soup
2 soup cans milk
1¼ cups (360 g) crunchy
    peanut butter

- Blend soup and milk in saucepan on medium heat.

- Stir in peanut butter and heat until it blends. Serve hot. Serves 4.

Chicken-Noodle Soup

1 85-g (3-ounce) package
   chicken-flavoured
   ramen noodles,
   broken
280 g (10 ounces) frozen green
   peas, thawed
1 115-g (4-ounce) jar sliced
   mushrooms
3 cups (420 g) cooked, cubed
   chicken

- Heat 2¼ cups (560 ml) water to boiling in large saucepan and add noodles, contents of seasoning packet and peas. (It's even better if you add 2 tablespoons (30 g) butter.)

- Heat to a boil; reduce heat to medium and cook for about 5 minutes.

- Stir in mushrooms, chicken and ¾ teaspoon pepper and continue cooking over medium heat until all ingredients heat through. Serves 6.

TIP: Garnish with about 1 cup (55 g) lightly crushed potato chips, if desired.

A team of scientists at the University of Nebraska has confirmed what grandmothers have known for centuries – that chicken soup is good for colds. Chicken soup contains several anti-inflammatory ingredients that affect the immune system.

Tasty Chicken and Rice Soup

450 g (1 pound) boneless skinless chicken breasts
½ cup (185 g) brown rice
1 280-g (10-ounce) can cream of chicken soup
1 280-g (10-ounce) can cream of celery soup
400 ml (14 ounces) chicken stock
1 teaspoon minced garlic
450 g (16 ounces) frozen sliced carrots, thawed
1 cup (250 ml) unthickened cream

- Cut chicken into 2-cm (1-inch) pieces.

- Place pieces in sprayed 4 to 5-L (4 to 5-quart) slow cooker.

- Mix rice, soups, chicken stock, garlic and carrots in bowl and pour over chicken.

- Cover and cook on low for 7 to 8 hours.

- Turn heat to high, add cream and cook for additional 15 to 20 minutes. Serves 6.

A wire whisk is super for blending canned soups and water.

Tortellini Soup

1 30-g (1-ounce) packet white
sauce mix
3 boneless, skinless
chicken breast halves
400 ml (14 ounces) chicken
stock
1 teaspoon minced garlic
½ teaspoon dried basil
½ teaspoon oregano
½ teaspoon cayenne
pepper
1 230-g (8-ounce) package
cheese tortellini
1½ cups (375 ml) unthickened
cream
6 cups (180 g) fresh baby spinach

- Place white sauce mix in
sprayed 5 to 6-L (5 to 6-quart)
slow cooker.

- Add 4 cups (1 L) water and
stir until mixture is smooth.
Cut chicken into 2-cm
(1-inch) pieces.

- Add chicken, stock, garlic, ½
teaspoon salt, basil, oregano and
cayenne pepper to mixture.

- Cover and cook on low for
6 to 7 hours or on high for
3 hours.

- Stir in pasta, cover and cook for
additional 1 hour on high.

- Stir in cream and fresh spinach
and cook just enough for soup to
get hot. Serves 6.

*TIP: Sprinkle a little shredded
parmesan cheese on top of
each serving as a nice touch.*

*In southern Italy, soup is said to relieve your hunger,
quench your thirst, fill your stomach, clean your teeth,
make you sleep, help you digest and colour your cheeks.*

Tortilla Soup

3 large boneless, skinless chicken breast halves, cubed
280 g (10 ounces) frozen corn, thawed
1 onion, chopped
1.2 L (2½ pints) chicken stock
170 g (6 ounces) tomato paste
2 280-g (10-ounce) cans tomatoes
60 g (2 ounces) green chillies, sliced
2 teaspoons ground cumin
1 teaspoon chilli powder
1 teaspoon salt
1 teaspoon minced garlic
6 corn tortillas

- Preheat oven to 190° C (375° F).

- Combine chicken, corn, onion, stock, tomato paste, tomatoes, green chillies, cumin, chilli powder, salt and garlic in large slow cooker.

- Cover and cook on low for 5 to 7 hours or on high for 3 to 3 hours 30 minutes.

- While soup is cooking, cut tortillas into ½-cm (¼-inch) strips and place on baking tray.

- Bake for about 5 minutes or until crisp.

- Serve baked tortilla strips with soup. Serves 6.

Big-Time Beef

Baked, Grilled, Fried and Cooked Slow and Easy

Big-Time Beef Contents

Barbecued Steak with Garlic-Mustard Sauce

⅓ cup (85 ml) apple juice
2 tablespoons (30 g)
    Dijon-style
    mustard
1 tablespoon (10 g) minced
    garlic
4 2-cm (1-inch) thick
    porterhouse steaks

- Combine apple juice, mustard, garlic and 1 teaspoon black pepper in bowl, and mix well. Remove and reserve ¼ cup (60 ml) sauce for basting. Brush steaks with remaining sauce.

- Grill steaks on barbecue over medium hot coals. Grill for about 15 to 18 minutes or until desired doneness and turn occasionally.

- During last 8 to 10 minutes of grilling, baste steaks with the ¼ cup (60 ml) sauce set aside for basting. Serves 4.

When buying fillets or steaks, be sure the meat is uniform in colour with no brown spots.

Marinated Blade Steak

1 340-ml (12-ounce) can cola
1 280-g (10-ounce) bottle
    teriyaki sauce
1.4 kg (3 pounds) blade steak

- Combine cola, teriyaki sauce and 1 teaspoon black pepper in large resealable plastic bag. Add steak, seal and marinate in refrigerator for 24 hours, turning occasionally.

- Remove steak from marinade and discard marinade. Grill, covered, for about 5 minutes on each side, or until meat reaches the desired pinkness.

- Let stand for about 10 minutes before slicing diagonally across grain. Serves 8.

Swiss Steak Dinner

450–680 g (1–1½ pounds)
    boneless, round steak
8–10 medium new
    (red) potatoes
    with peels, halved
1 cup (120 g) baby carrots
1 onion, sliced
1 425-g (15-ounce) can
    tomatoes
340 g (12 ounces) beef gravy

- Cut steak in 6 to 8 serving-size pieces, season with ½ teaspoon each of salt and pepper and brown in non-stick frypan. Layer steak pieces, potatoes, carrots and onion in slow cooker.

- Combine tomatoes and beef gravy in saucepan and spoon over vegetables. Cover and cook on low for 7 to 8 hours. Serves 6 to 8.

Steak and Potatoes

900 g (2 pounds) round steak
⅓ cup (40 g) flour
⅓ cup (85 ml) canola oil
5 peeled potatoes, diced
¼ cup (40 g) chopped onions
1 280-g (10-ounce) can cream of
** mushroom soup**

- Preheat oven to 175° C (350° F).

- Cut steak into serving-size pieces and coat in flour. Brown with oil in heavy frypan and drain. Place steak in sprayed 23 x 33-cm (9 x 13-inch) baking dish.

- Season potatoes with a little salt and pepper, place over steak and cover with onions and mushroom soup diluted with ½ cup (125 ml) water. Cover and bake for 1 hour 30 minutes. Serves 8.

Fried Steak and Veggies

450 g (1 pound) boneless
** sirloin steak,**
** cut into strips**
Canola oil
2 425-g (15-ounce) cans
** Italian tomatoes**
** with juice**
450 g (16 ounces) frozen
** green beans, thawed**
230 g (8 ounces) sour cream
Noodles, cooked

- Place sirloin strips in large frypan with a little oil. Cook on high heat for about 3 minutes.

- Add tomatoes and green beans, bring to a boil, lower heat and cook for 10 minutes.

- Just before serving, fold in sour cream. Serve over noodles. Serves 6.

Zesty Rice and Beef

450 g (1 pound) lean minced
    round steak
1 onion, chopped
1 green capsicum,
    chopped
2½ cups (415 g) cooked rice
1 425-g (15-ounce) can
    corn, drained
2 425-g (15-ounce) cans
    tomatoes
1 teaspoon Mexican seasoning
2 teaspoons chilli powder
1 teaspoon garlic powder
230 g (8 ounces) package
    cubed processed
    cheese
1 cup (60 g) buttery cracker
    crumbs
½ cup (55 g) chopped pecans
    or walnuts
2 tablespoons (30 g) butter,
    melted

- Preheat oven to 175° C (350° F).

- Cook beef, onion and capsicum
  in large frypan or roasting pan
  over medium heat until beef is
  no longer pink. Drain well.

- Add rice, corn, tomatoes,
  seasoning, chilli powder, garlic
  powder and ½ teaspoon salt and
  bring to a boil. Remove from
  heat.

- Add cheese and stir until cheese
  melts. Spoon into sprayed
  23 x 33-cm (9 x 13-inch) baking
  dish. Combine cracker crumbs,
  pecans and butter in bowl.
  Sprinkle over top of casserole.
  Bake for 25 minutes or until
  casserole is bubbly hot.
  Serves 8.

Thai Beef, Noodles and Veggies

2 130-g (4½-ounce) packages
  Thai noodles
450 g (1 pound) sirloin steak,
  cut into strips
Canola oil
450 g (16 ounces)
  frozen stir-fry
  vegetables, thawed
½ cup (85 g) chopped
  peanuts

- Cook noodles according to package directions and remove from heat. Place in serving bowl, cover and keep warm.

- Season sirloin strips with a little salt and pepper.

- Brown half sirloin strips in a little oil in frypan and cook for about 2 minutes. Remove from frypan and drain.

- Add remaining sirloin strips, brown in frypan with a little oil and cook for about 2 minutes. Remove from frypan and drain.

- In same frypan, place vegetables and ½ cup (125 ml) water, cover and cook for 5 minutes or until tender but crisp.

- Remove from heat, add steak strips and toss to mix.

- Spoon over warm noodles to serve; sprinkle with peanuts. Serves 6.

Natural peanut butter is made without sugar or hydrogenated oils and has a thicker texture than processed peanut butter.

On-the-Border Steak

½ teaspoon dry mustard
2 tablespoons (20 g) taco
   seasoning
1 teaspoon minced garlic
680 g (1½ pounds) sirloin steak
Canola oil
1 cup (265 g) chunky salsa,
   heated
Rice, cooked

- Combine ½ teaspoon pepper, dry mustard, taco seasoning and garlic in bowl. Rub sirloin steak with a little oil, sprinkle seasonings over steak and refrigerate for 4 to 6 hours.

- Grill steak on each side, covered, for 6 to 8 minutes on medium heat. Cut steak diagonally across grain into thin strips.

- Serve with hot salsa and spoon over rice. Serves 6.

Sizzling Sirloin

2 teaspoons canola oil
2 teaspoons minced garlic
½ teaspoon cayenne
   pepper
2 tablespoons (30 ml) soy sauce
2 tablespoons (30 ml) honey
450 g (1 pound) beef sirloin,
   thinly sliced
Rice, cooked

- Combine oil, garlic, cayenne pepper, soy sauce and honey and place in resealable plastic bag.

- Add sliced beef, seal bag and shake. Refrigerate for 30 minutes.

- Place beef mixture in large sprayed frypan over medium-high heat. Cook for 5 to 6 minutes or until desired doneness, but do not over-cook. Serve over rice. Serves 6.

Seasoned-Beef Tenderloin

3 tablespoons (40 g) Dijon-style
mustard
2 tablespoons (30 g) horseradish
1.4 kg (3 pounds) centre-cut
beef tenderloin
½ cup (60 g) seasoned
breadcrumbs

- Combine mustard and
horseradish in bowl and
spread over beef tenderloin.

- Spread breadcrumbs onto
horseradish-mustard mixture and
wrap beef in foil. Refrigerate for
at least 12 hours.

- When ready to bake, preheat
oven to 190° C (375° F).

- Remove wrap and place on
sprayed baking tray. Bake for
30 minutes. Let tenderloin stand
for 15 minutes before slicing.
Serves 8 to 10.

Steak with Creamy Horseradish Sauce

900 g (2 pounds) sirloin steak
230 g (8 ounces) sour
cream
¼ cup (60 g) horseradish

- Preheat griller. Pat steak dry and
sprinkle liberally with salt and
pepper.

- Grill steak on rack about
8 cm (3 inches) from heat
for about 5 minutes on both
sides. Let stand for 5 minutes
before slicing.

- Combine sour cream,
horseradish and a little salt
and pepper in bowl and mix
well. Serve with steak. Serves 8.

Old-Fashioned Pot Roast

1 1-kg (2-pound) boneless rump roast
5 medium potatoes, peeled, quartered
450 g (16 ounces) peeled baby carrots
2 medium onions, quartered
1 280-g (10-ounce) can golden mushroom soup
½ teaspoon dried basil

- Brown roast in frypan on all sides. Place potatoes, carrots and onions in sprayed 4 to 5-L (4 to 5-quart) slow cooker.

- Place browned roast on top of vegetables.

- Combine soup, basil and ½ teaspoon salt in bowl and pour mixture over meat and vegetables.

- Cover and cook on low for 9 to 11 hours. Serves 8.

TIP: To serve, transfer roast and vegetables to serving plate. Stir juices remaining in slow cooker and spoon over roast and vegetables.

O'Brian's Hash

3 cups (420 g) cubed, cooked
 beef roast
800 g (28 ounces) frozen
 hash browns, thawed
 and shredded
100 g (3½ ounces) green
 capsicum, diced
50 g (2 ounces) onion, finely
 sliced
Canola oil
450 g (16 ounces) salsa
1 tablespoon (10 g) beef
 seasoning
1 cup (115 g) shredded
 cheddar cheese

- Place cubed beef in large, sprayed
 slow cooker.

- Brown potatoes, capsicum and
 onion in a little oil in large frypan
 and transfer to slow cooker. Stir in
 salsa and beef seasoning.

- Cover and cook on high for
 4 to 5 hours.

- When ready to serve, sprinkle
 cheese over hash. Serves 8.

All-the-Trimmings Corned Beef

1.8–2.2 kg (4–5 pounds)
 corned silverside
4 large potatoes,
 peeled, quartered
6 carrots, peeled, halved
4 onions
1 head cabbage

- Place corned beef in roasting
 pan, cover with water and bring
 to a boil. Turn heat down and
 simmer for 3 hours. (Add water
 if necessary.)

- Add potatoes, carrots and
 onions. Cut cabbage into eighths
 and lay over top of
 other vegetables.

- Bring to a boil, turn heat
 down and cook for additional
 30 to 40 minutes until
 vegetables are done. When
 slightly cool, slice corned beef
 across grain. Serves 8 to 10.

Beef Patties with Mushroom Gravy

450 g (1 pound) lean
   minced beef
¼ cup (70 g) chilli sauce
1 egg, beaten
¾ cup (20 g) crushed
   cornflakes
Canola oil
2 280-g (10-ounce) cans
   cream of
   mushroom soup

- Combine beef, chilli sauce, egg, cornflakes and a little salt and pepper in bowl and mix well. Shape into 4 patties, about 2 cm (¾ inch) thick.

- Place patties in frypan with a little oil and brown each patty on high heat.

- Reduce heat, cover and simmer for 10 to 15 minutes.

- Combine soup with ½ cup (125 ml) water in bowl and mix well.

- Spoon mixture over patties and simmer for about 10 minutes. Serves 4.

TIP: This gravy is great served over mashed potatoes or hot dumplings.

When purchasing minced beef, remember that fat greatly contributes to its flavour. The lower the fat content, the drier it will be once cooked.

Taco Bueno Bake

900 g (2 pounds) minced beef
1½ cups (410 g) taco sauce
2 115-g (4-ounce) packets
  Spanish rice
230 g (8 ounces) shredded
  cheddar cheese blend

- Preheat oven to 175° C (350° F).

- Brown beef in frypan and drain. Prepare rice according to packet directions and add to pan, along with taco sauce and half cheese. Spoon mixture into sprayed 3-L (3-quart) baking dish.

- Cover and bake for 35 minutes. Uncover and sprinkle remaining cheese on top and return to oven for 5 minutes. Serves 8.

Simple Casserole Dinner

450 g (1 pound) lean
  minced beef
¼ cup (25 g) white rice
1 280-g (10-ounce) can French
  onion soup
170 g (6 ounces) onion, finely
  sliced and fried until crispy

- Preheat oven to 160° C (325° F).

- Brown beef, drain and place in sprayed 18 x 28-cm (7 x 11-inch) baking dish. Add rice, onion soup and ½ cup (125 ml) water.

- Cover and bake for 40 minutes. Uncover, sprinkle onion over top and return to oven for 10 minutes. Serves 6.

Frypan Beef and Pasta

170 g (8 ounces) spiral
    pasta
400 ml (14 ounces) beef
    stock
450 g (1 pound) lean minced
    beef
620 g (22 ounces) tinned corn
100 g (3½ ounces) red capsicum,
    diced
340 g (12 ounces) cubed
    processed cheese

- Cook pasta in 4¼ cups (1.1 L) water with beef stock added.

- While pasta cooks, brown beef in large frypan, stir and drain.

- Stir in corn, capsicum and cheese and cook on low heat until cheese melts.

- Gently stir cooked pasta into beef mixture until it coats pasta.

- Spoon mixture into serving bowl and garnish with few sprigs parsley, if desired. Serves 8.

*Stock is a strained, thin, clear liquid in which
meat, poultry or fish simmers with vegetables and herbs.
Make your own or shop for reduced salt, low-fat packaged stock.*

Slow-Cook Beef Pasta

**680 g (1½ pounds) lean
minced beef
400 g (14 ounces) frozen
capsicum, thawed
100 g (3½ ounces) diced onion
450 g (16 ounces) cubed
processed cheese
2 425-g (15-ounce) cans
tomatoes, with
liquid
1 tablespoon (5 g) fresh coriander
1 tablespoon (15 ml) lemon juice
2 425-g (15-ounce) cans
corn, drained
230 g (8 ounces) fettuccini
(medium egg noodles)
1 cup (115 g) shredded
cheddar cheese
Fresh parsley or spring onions
(optional)**

- Brown beef in frypan and drain fat. Place beef in 5 to 6-L (5 to 6-quart) slow cooker, add capsicum, onions, cheese, tomatoes, coriander, lemon juice, corn and about ½ teaspoon salt and mix well. Cover and cook on low for 4 to 5 hours.

- Cook pasta according to package directions, drain and fold into beef-tomato mixture.

- Cook for additional 30 minutes to heat thoroughly.

- When ready to serve, top with cheddar cheese, several sprinkles of chopped fresh parsley or chopped spring onions, if you like. Serves 8.

Tex-Mex Dinner

450 g (1 pound) lean minced beef
1 large onion, chopped
1 425-g (15-ounce) can borlotti
beans, drained
1½ teaspoons cumin
½ head lettuce, torn
2 tomatoes, chopped
1 avocado, diced
3 spring onions, chopped
230 g (8 ounces) shredded
cheddar cheese
280 g (10 ounces) corn
chips, slightly crushed
170 ml (6 ounces) Thousand
Island salad dressing

- Sauté beef and onion in frypan. Drain grease, add beans, cumin and 1 cup (250 ml) water and simmer until water is absorbed.

- Combine lettuce, tomatoes, avocado and spring onions in large bowl.

- When ready to serve, add warm beef mixture, cheese, chips and dressing, and toss. Serve immediately. Serves 8.

Oriental Beef and Noodles

570 g (1¼ pounds) minced beef
2 85-g (3-ounce) packages
   Oriental-flavoured
   ramen noodles, broken up
450 g (16 ounces) frozen
   stir-fry vegetables
½ teaspoon ground
   ginger
3 tablespoons (20 g) thinly
   sliced spring onions

- Brown beef in large frypan and drain.

- Add ½ cup (125 ml) water and a little salt and pepper to beef in frypan, simmer for 10 minutes and transfer to separate bowl.

- In same frypan, combine 2 cups (500 ml) water, noodles (with seasoning), vegetables and ginger.

- Bring to boil and reduce heat.

- Cover and simmer for 3 minutes or until noodles are tender and stir once.

- Return beef to frypan and stir in spring onions. Serve right from frypan. Serves 8.

It takes about 60 grams of dry pasta to make 1 cup of cooked pasta. Spaghetti and macaroni products usually double in volume when cooked. Egg noodles don't expand quite as much.

Easy Meat 'n' Potatoes

450 g (1 pound) minced beef
1 280-g (10-ounce) can
    bolognaise sauce
200 g (7 ounces) processed
    cheese spread
80 g (3 ounces) chilli salsa
900 g (32 ounces) frozen
    hash browns, thawed
    and shredded

- Preheat oven to 205° C (400° F).

- Brown beef in frypan over
  medium heat and drain. Add
  bolognaise sauce, cheese spread
  and salsa to beef and mix well.

- Place hash browns in sprayed
  23 x 33-cm (9 x 13-inch) baking
  dish and top with beef mixture.
  Cover and bake for 25 minutes.
  Uncover and bake for additional
  10 minutes. Serves 6.

TIP: This is really good sprinkled
    with 1 cup (115 g) shredded
    cheddar cheese.

Chilli Casserole

2 500-g (20-ounce) cans chilli
    with beans
1 115-g (4-ounce) jar chopped
    green chillies
60 g (2 ounces) sliced
    black olives
230 g (8 ounces) shredded
    cheddar cheese
2 cups (120 g) Mexican-flavoured
    corn chips, crushed

- Preheat oven to 175° C (350° F).

- Combine all ingredients in bowl
  and transfer to sprayed 3-L
  (3-quart) baking dish.

- Bake for 35 minutes or until it
  bubbles. Serves 8.

Cowboy's Tin Plate Supper

680 g (1½ pounds) lean minced beef
2 onions, coarsely chopped
5 medium potatoes, peeled and sliced
1 425-g (15-ounce) can kidney beans, rinsed and drained
1 425-g (15-ounce) can borlotti beans, drained
1 425-g (15-ounce) can tomatoes
1 280-g (10-ounce) can tomato soup
Fresh coriander (to taste)
Lemon juice (to taste)
½ teaspoon basil
½ teaspoon oregano
2 teaspoons minced garlic

- Sprinkle beef with a little salt and pepper in frypan, brown beef and drain.

- Place onions in slow cooker and spoon beef over onions.

- On top of beef, layer potatoes, kidney beans and borlotti beans.

- Pour tomatoes and tomato soup over beans and potatoes.

- Sprinkle with coriander, lemon juice, basil, oregano and garlic.

- Cover and cook on low for 7 to 8 hours. Serves 8 to 10.

The round white potato and the round red potato are both best suited for boiling. The round white potato has a speckled brown skin and the round red has a red skin. Both have less starch than baking potatoes and more moisture. They are also well suited to mashed potatoes.

Ravioli and More

450 g (1 pound) lean minced beef
1 teaspoon garlic powder
1 large onion, chopped
2 grated zucchinis
¼ cup (60 g) butter
1 740-g (26-ounce) jar spaghetti
   sauce
1 570-g (20-ounce) package
   mushroom ravioli, cooked
340 g (12 ounces)
   shredded mozzarella
   cheese

- Preheat oven to 175° C (350° F).

- Brown beef in large frypan until no longer pink and drain. Add garlic powder and ½ teaspoon each of salt and pepper.

- Cook onion and zucchini with butter in saucepan just until tender but crisp and stir in spaghetti sauce. Spread ½ cup (135 g) sauce in sprayed 23 x 33-cm (9 x 13-inch) baking dish.

- Layer half pasta, half spaghetti sauce, half beef and half cheese. Repeat layers, but save remaining cheese for topping.

- Cover and bake for 35 minutes. Uncover and sprinkle remaining cheese on top. Let stand for 10 minutes before serving. Serves 8.

Cheesy Stuffed Capsicums

In just about every casserole we make, we use capsicums, but with this recipe you get the whole capsicum with just the right 'stuff' to make it delicious.

6 green capsicums
680 g (1½ pounds) lean minced beef
½ cup (80 g) chopped onion
¾ cup (125 g) cooked rice
1 egg
2 425-g (15-ounce) cans Italian tomatoes
½ teaspoon garlic powder
1 tablespoon (15 ml) Worcestershire sauce
230 g (8 ounces) shredded cheddar cheese

- Preheat oven to 175° C (350° F).

- Cut off small portion of tops of capsicum and remove seeds and membranes. Place in roasting pan with salted water and boil. Cook for 10 minutes so they will be only partially done. Drain and set aside to cool.

- Brown beef and onion in frypan and drain. Add rice, egg, 1 can tomatoes, garlic powder, Worcestershire sauce and about ½ teaspoon each of salt and pepper. Simmer for 5 minutes. Remove from heat and add 1 cup (115 g) cheese and mix well.

- Stuff capsicums with meat mixture and sit upright in sprayed, round baking dish. (You may have to trim little slivers off bottoms of capsicums so they will sit upright.) Pour remaining can of tomatoes over top and around capsicums.

- Bake for 25 minutes. Remove from oven, sprinkle remaining cheese on top and return to oven for 10 minutes until cheese melts. Serves 6.

Super Spaghetti Pie

This is a great recipe to make ahead of time and have ready for dinner or a midnight supper when teenagers demand 'food'! And, it even resembles pizza.

230 g (8 ounces) spaghetti
⅓ cup (35 g) grated parmesan
   cheese
1 egg, beaten
1 tablespoon (15 g) butter,
   melted
1 cup (225 g) cottage
   cheese, drained
230 g (½ pound) lean minced beef
230 g (½ pound) salami
½ cup (80 g) chopped onion
1 425-g (15-ounce) jar tomato
   simmer sauce
1 teaspoon garlic powder
1 teaspoon oregano
½ cup (60 g) shredded
   mozzarella cheese

- Preheat oven to 175° C (350° F).

- Cook pasta according to package directions. While pasta is still warm, stir in parmesan cheese, egg and butter in large bowl.

- Pour into sprayed 25-cm (10-inch) pie dish and pat mixture up and around sides with spoon to form a crust. Pour cottage cheese over spaghetti crust.

- Brown beef, salami and onion in frypan. Drain off fat and add simmer sauce, garlic powder, oregano and ½ teaspoon each of salt and pepper. Simmer for 10 minutes and stir occasionally.

- Pour meat mixture over cottage cheese. Bake for 30 minutes. Arrange mozzarella on top and return to oven until cheese melts. Serves 8.

Beef and Pasta

900 g (2 pounds) lean, minced
   beef
2 onions, chopped
1 green capsicum,
   chopped
¾ teaspoon garlic powder
1 400-g (14-ounce) jar spaghetti
   sauce
1 425-g (15-ounce) can Italian
   tomatoes
1 115-g (4-ounce) can sliced
   mushrooms, drained
230 g (8 ounces) spiral pasta
680 g (1½ pints) sour cream
230 g (8 ounces) sliced
   provolone cheese
230 g (8 ounces) shredded
   mozzarella cheese

- Preheat oven to 160° C (325° F).

- Brown and cook beef in deep frypan and stir often to break up pieces. Drain off excess fat.

- Add onions, capsicum, garlic powder, spaghetti sauce, tomatoes and mushrooms and mix well. Simmer for 20 minutes.

- Cook pasta according to package directions and drain. Pour half pasta into sprayed 30 x 36-cm (11 x 14-inch) baking dish.

- Cover with half meat-tomato mixture and half sour cream. Top with half provolone cheese. Repeat process once more.

- Cover and bake for 35 minutes.

- Remove cover and sprinkle mozzarella cheese and continue baking for additional 5 minutes or until cheese melts. Serves 10.

Spaghetti Bake

230 g (8 ounces) spaghetti
450 g (1 pound) lean minced beef
1 green capsicum, finely
    chopped
1 onion, chopped
1 280-g (10-ounce) can tomato
    soup
1 485-g (15-ounce) jar tomato
    simmer sauce
⅓ cup (80 ml) water
½ teaspoon salt
2 teaspoons Italian
    seasoning
1 230-g (8-ounce) can
    corn, drained
115 g (4 ounces) sliced black
    olives, drained
340 g (12 ounces)
    shredded cheddar
    cheese

- Cook pasta according to package directions, drain and set aside. Cook beef, capsicum and onion in frypan and drain.

- Add remaining ingredients plus ⅓ cup (75 ml) water, ½ teaspoon salt and pasta to beef mixture and stir well. Pour into sprayed 23 x 33-cm (9 x 13-inch) baking dish and cover.

- Refrigerate for 2 to 3 hours.

- When ready to bake, preheat oven to 175° C (350° F). Cover and bake for 45 minutes. Serves 8.

Enchilada Lasagna

680 g (1½ pounds) lean minced
    beef
1 onion, chopped
1 teaspoon minced
    garlic
1 425-g (15-ounce) jar
    enchilada or taco sauce
1 425-g (15-ounce) can
    tomatoes
1 teaspoon cumin
1 egg
1½ cups (340 g) cottage cheese
200 g (7 ounces) shredded
    mozzarella cheese
150 g (5 ounces) shredded
    parmesan cheese
8 20-cm (8-inch) corn
    tortillas, torn
1 cup (115 g) shredded
    cheddar cheese

- Preheat oven to 160° C (325° F).

- Cook beef, onion and garlic in large frypan until meat is no longer pink. Stir in enchilada sauce, tomatoes, cumin and ½ teaspoon salt. Bring mixture to a boil, reduce heat and simmer for 20 minutes.

- Combine egg and cottage cheese in small bowl. Spread one-third of meat sauce into sprayed 23 x 33-cm (9 x 13-inch) baking dish. Top with half mozzarella and half parmesan, tortillas and cottage cheese mixture. Repeat layers.

- Top with remaining meat sauce and sprinkle with cheddar cheese. Cover and bake for 25 minutes. Uncover and bake for additional 10 minutes. Serves 8.

Taco Pie

450 g (1 pound) lean minced beef
½ capsicum, chopped
2 jalapeno chillies,
    seeded and chopped
Canola oil
1 425-g (15-ounce) can tomatoes
1 teaspoon chilli powder
1 tablespoon (5 g) fresh coriander
1 tablespoon (15 ml) lemon juice
230 g (8 ounces) shredded sharp
    cheddar cheese
1 170-g (6-ounce) package
    scone mix
1 egg
⅓ cup (85 ml) milk

- Preheat oven to 190° C (375° F).

- Brown beef, capsicum and jalapeno chillies in a little oil in large frypan and drain well. Add ½ teaspoon salt, tomatoes, 1 cup (250 ml) water, chilli powder, coriander and lemon juice. Cook on medium heat for about 10 minutes or until most liquid cooks out, but mixture is not dry.

- Pour into sprayed 23 x 33-cm (9 x 13-inch) glass baking dish. Sprinkle cheese on top.

- Combine scone mix, egg and milk in bowl and beat well. Pour over top of cheese.

- Bake for 25 minutes or until scone mix is light brown.

- Remove from oven and set aside for about 10 minutes before serving. Serves 8.

TIP: If you want to make this a day ahead, put everything together except scone mixture. Mix the dough just before you are ready to bake the Taco Pie.

Dinner's Ready

450 g (1 pound) lean minced beef
1 onion, chopped
4 tablespoons (70 g) steak sauce
1 tablespoon (10 g) flour
1 425-g (15-ounce) can baked
  beans with liquid
1 230-g (8-ounce) can
  corn, drained
1½ cups (60 g) garlic-flavoured
  croutons, crushed

- Preheat oven to 160° C (325° F).

- Brown beef and onion in
  large frypan and drain. Stir
  in remaining ingredients
  except croutons.

- Pour into sprayed 23 x 33-cm
  (9 x 13-inch) baking dish.
  Sprinkle crouton crumbs on top.

- Bake for 45 minutes or until
  bubbly around edges. Serves 8.

TIP: You can make this ahead of
  time and freeze. When you
  need it, just thaw and cook.

Spiced Beef

450 g (1 pound) lean minced beef
1 30-g (1-ounce) packet taco
  seasoning mix
1 425-g (15-ounce) can
  tomatoes with liquid
Fresh coriander (to taste)
Lemon juice (to taste)
1 425-g (15-ounce) can kidney
  beans with liquid
450 g (1 pound) fettuccini (egg
  noodles)

- Cook beef in frypan and drain.
  Add taco seasoning and ½ cup
  (125 ml) water and simmer for
  15 minutes.

- Add tomatoes, coriander, lemon
  juice and kidney beans. (You
  may need to add ¼ teaspoon
  salt.)

- Cook pasta according to package
  directions and serve beef over
  pasta. Serves 6.

Super-Duper Dinner

900 g (2 pounds) lean minced beef
1 onion, chopped
1 900-g (2-pound) package frozen potato gems
230 g (8 ounces) shredded cheddar cheese
2 280-g (10-ounce) cans cream of mushroom soup
1 soup can milk

- Preheat oven to 175° C (350° F).

- Crumble beef into sprayed 23 x 33-cm (9 x 13-inch) glass baking dish. Sprinkle with a little salt and pepper.

- Cover with onion. Top with potato gems and sprinkle with cheese.

- Combine soups and milk in saucepan. Heat and stir just enough to mix in milk. Pour over casserole.

- Bake covered for 1 hour. Uncover and bake for additional 15 minutes. Serves 8.

Large scooped-out vegetables, round loaves of bread hollowed out or foil-lined flowerpots make good serving dishes for dips.

Chilli Relleno Casserole

450 g (1 pound) lean
   minced beef
1 capsicum, chopped
1 onion, chopped
1 115-g (4-ounce) jar
   chopped green chillies
1 teaspoon oregano
1 teaspoon dried
   coriander leaves
¾ teaspoon garlic powder
1 230-g (8-ounce) jar whole
   green chillies
1½ cups (170 g) shredded
   Colby cheese
1½ cups (170 g) shredded
   sharp cheddar cheese
3 large eggs
1 tablespoon (10 g) flour
1 cup (250 ml) unthickened
   cream

- Preheat oven to 175° C (350° F).

- Cook meat with capsicum and onion in frypan. Add chopped green chillies, oregano, coriander, garlic powder and about ½ teaspoon each of salt and pepper.

- Seed whole chillies and spread into sprayed 23 x 33-cm (9 x 13-inch) baking dish. Cover with meat mixture and sprinkle with cheeses.

- Combine eggs and flour in bowl and beat with fork until fluffy. Add cream, mix and pour slowly over top of meat in casserole. Bake for 35 minutes or until it is light brown. Serves 8.

Cabbage Rolls Along

This is a wonderful family recipe and a super way to get the kids to eat cabbage. Everyone who has ever had a garden has probably made some version of these well-loved cabbage rolls.

**1 large head cabbage,
    cored**
**680 g (1½ pounds) lean
    minced beef**
1 egg, beaten
3 tablespoons (45 g) tomato sauce
**⅓ cup (40 g) seasoned
    breadcrumbs**
**2 tablespoons (20 g) dried
    minced onion flakes**
**2 425-g (15-ounce) cans
    Italian tomatoes**
¼ cup (30 g) cornflour
**3 tablespoons (45 g) brown
    sugar**
**2 tablespoons (30 ml)
    Worcestershire
    sauce**

- Preheat oven to 160° C (325° F).

- Place head of cabbage in large soup pot of boiling water for 10 minutes or until outer leaves are tender. Drain well. Rinse in cold water and remove 10 large outer leaves*. Set aside.

- Slice or shred remaining cabbage. Place into sprayed 23 x 33-cm (9 x 13-inch) baking dish.

- Combine beef, egg, sauce, breadcrumbs, onion flakes and 1 teaspoon salt in large bowl and mix well.

- Pack together about ½ cup (70 g) meat mixture and put on each cabbage leaf. Fold in sides and roll leaf to completely enclose filling. (You may have to remove thick vein from cabbage leaves for easier rolling.) Place each rolled leaf over shredded cabbage.

continued next page...

- Place tomatoes in large saucepan. Combine cornflour, brown sugar and Worcestershire sauce in bowl and spoon mixture into tomatoes. Cook on high heat, stirring constantly until stewed tomatoes and juices thicken. Pour over cabbage rolls. Cover and bake for 1 hour. Serves 10.

TIP: To get that many large leaves, you may have to put 2 smaller leaves together to make one roll.

Shepherds' Pie

450 g (1 pound) lean minced beef
1 30-g (1-ounce) packet taco seasoning mix
1 cup (115 g) shredded cheddar cheese
1 230-g (8-ounce) can corn, drained
2 cups (420 g) cooked instant mashed potatoes

- Preheat oven to 175° C (350° F).

- Brown beef in frypan, cook for 10 minutes and drain. Add taco seasoning and ¾ cup (175 ml) water and cook for an additional 5 minutes.

- Spoon beef mixture into 20-cm (8-inch) baking pan, sprinkle cheese on top. Sprinkle with corn and spread mashed potatoes over top. Bake for 25 minutes or until top is golden. Serves 5.

Enchilada Casserole

**680 g (1½ pounds) lean
   minced beef
1 30-g (1-ounce) package taco
   seasoning mix
Canola oil
8 flour or corn tortillas
1 cup (115 g) shredded cheddar
   cheese, divided
1 onion, chopped
1 280-g (10-ounce) can
   enchilada or taco sauce
1 200-g (7-ounce) jar green
   chillies
1½ cups (170 g) shredded
   mozzarella cheese
230 g (8 ounces) sour
   cream**

- Preheat oven to 175° C (350° F).

- Brown beef in frypan with a
  little salt and pepper until it
  crumbles and is brown. Drain
  well.

- Add taco seasoning mix and
  1¼ cups (310 g) water to beef
  and simmer for 5 minutes.

- In separate frypan pour just
  enough oil to cover bottom of
  frypan and heat until it is hot.

- Cook tortillas one at a time,
  until soft and limp, for about
  5 to 10 seconds on each side.
  Drain on paper towels.

- After you cook tortillas, spoon
  ⅓ cup (50 g) meat mixture into
  centre of each tortilla. Sprinkle
  with small amount of cheddar
  cheese and 1 spoonful of
  chopped onion. Roll and place
  seam-side down in sprayed
  23 x 33-cm (9 x 13-inch) baking
  dish.

- After filling all tortillas, add
  enchilada sauce and green
  chillies to remaining meat
  mixture. Spoon over tortillas.
  Cover and bake for about
  30 minutes.

- Uncover and sprinkle remaining
  cheddar cheese and mozzarella
  cheese over casserole.

- Return to oven just until cheese
  melts. Place dabs of sour cream
  over enchiladas to serve. Serves 8.

Quick Fry

**680 g (1½ pounds) lean
 minced beef**
⅔ cup (180 g) stir-fry sauce
**450 g (16 ounces) frozen
 stir-fry vegetables**
**2 85-g (3-ounce) packages
 Oriental-flavour
 ramen noodles**

- Brown and crumble beef in large frypan. Add 2½ cups (625 ml) water, stir-fry sauce, vegetables and seasoning packets from ramen noodles.

- Cook and stir on medium-low heat for about 5 minutes.

- Break noodles, add to beef-vegetable mixture and cook for about 6 minutes. Stir to separate noodles as they soften. Serves 8.

Potato and Beef Casserole

**4 medium potatoes,
 peeled and sliced**
**570 g (1¼ pounds) lean minced
 beef, browned and
 drained**
**1 280-g (10-ounce) can cream
 of mushroom soup**
**1 280-g (10-ounce) can
 vegetable beef soup**

- Preheat oven to 175° C (350° F).

- Combine all ingredients in large bowl. Add a little salt and pepper. Transfer to sprayed 3-L (3-quart) baking dish. Cover and bake for 1 hour 30 minutes or until potatoes are tender. Serves 4 to 6.

Borlotti Bean Pie

450 g (1 pound) lean
   minced beef
1 onion, chopped
2 425-g (15-ounce) cans
   borlotti beans with
   liquid
1 280-g (10-ounce) can
   tomatoes with liquid
60 g (2 ounces) sliced green
   chillies
85 g (3 ounces) onions, finely
   sliced and fried until crispy

- Preheat oven to 175° C (350° F).

- Brown beef and onion in frypan
and drain. Layer 1 can beans,
beef-onion mixture, half can
tomatoes and half green chillies
in 2-L (2-quart) baking dish,
then repeat layer.

- Top with onion and bake for
30 minutes. Serves 6.

Extra Special Queso con Carne

*('Queso con Carne' means 'cheese
with meat'.)*

450 g (1 pound) lean minced beef
600 g (20 ounces) salsa
300 g (10 ounces) processed
   cheese spread
1 425-g (15-ounce) can kidney
   beans, rinsed, drained
Corn chips

- Cook beef over medium heat in
frypan and stir in salsa, cheese
and beans.

- Bring mixture to a boil and stir
constantly. Reduce heat to low
and simmer for 5 minutes.

- Serve with corn chips. Serves 8.

Beef Picante

This is a good family dish, and you can take the frypan right to the table.

450 g (1 pound) lean minced beef
1 280-g (10-ounce) can tomato soup
1 cup (265 g) chunky salsa
6 15-cm (6-inch) flour tortillas, cut into 2-cm (1-inch) pieces
1¼ cups (145 g) shredded cheddar cheese

- Cook beef in frypan until brown and drain.

- Add soup, salsa, ¾ cup (175 ml) water, tortillas, ½ teaspoon salt and half cheese. Heat to a boil. Cover and cook over low heat for 5 minutes.

- Top with remaining cheese. Serve straight from frypan. Serves 4 to 5.

Cheese may be frozen. Processed cheeses will last 4 months frozen and cheddar or other natural cheese will keep about 6 weeks when properly wrapped. Thaw all cheese overnight in refrigerator and use soon after thawing.

Cheeseburger Dinner

150 g (5 ounces) finely sliced
    white potatoes
60 g (2 ounces) parmesan cheese
60 g (2 ounces) bacon, finely
    diced and fried until crispy
⅓ cup (85 ml) milk
¼ cup (60 g) butter, melted
680 g (1½ pounds) lean minced
    beef
1 onion, coarsely chopped
Canola oil
1 425-g (15-ounce) can
    corn with liquid
230 g (8 ounces) shredded
    cheddar cheese

- Place potatoes, parmesan cheese and bacon in sprayed slow cooker.

- Pour 2¼ cups (560 ml) boiling water, milk and butter over potatoes.

- Brown beef and onion in a little oil in frypan, drain and spoon over potatoes. Top with corn.

- Cover and cook on low for 6 to 7 hours.

- When ready to serve, sprinkle cheese over corn. Serves 4 to 6.

Corned Beef Dinner

1.8–2.3 kg (4–5 pounds) corned silverside
4 large potatoes, peeled and quartered
6 carrots, peeled and halved
1 head cabbage

- Place silverside in roasting pan and cover with water. Bring to a boil. Turn heat down and simmer for 3 hours. Add water, if necessary.

- Add potatoes and carrots around meat. Cut cabbage into eighths and lay over top of potatoes and carrots.

- Bring to a boil, turn heat down and cook for additional 30 to 40 minutes or until vegetables are tender. Slice corned beef across the grain. Serves 8.

TIP: Leftover corned beef is great on sandwiches.

Corned beef is beef that is cured in a salt brine, often with spices.

Corny Chilli and Beans

2 425-g (15-ounce) cans chilli
  with beans
1 425-g (15-ounce) can
  tomatoes
1 310-g (11-ounce) can
  corn, drained
1 tablespoon (10 g) Mexican
  seasoning
1 tablespoon (30 ml) lemon juice
1 tablespoon (5 g) coriander
2 diced ripe avocados

• Combine chilli, tomatoes, corn,
  seasoning, lemon juice and
  coriander in microwave-safe
  bowl. Cover loosely and cook on
  high in microwave for about
  4 minutes.

• Stir in diced avocados and serve
  hot. Serves 6.

Reuben Hotdogs

1 780-g (27-ounce) can
  sauerkraut, rinsed and
  drained
2 teaspoons caraway seeds
8 hotdogs, halved lengthwise
1 cup (110 g) shredded Swiss
  cheese
Thousand Island salad
  dressing

• Preheat oven to 175° C (350° F).

• Place sauerkraut in sprayed 2-L
  (2-quart) baking dish. Sprinkle
  caraway seeds over top and add
  hotdogs.

• Bake for 20 minutes or until
  they are hot. Sprinkle with
  cheese. Bake for additional
  3 to 5 minutes or until cheese
  melts. Serve with salad dressing.
  Serves 6.

Reuben Casserole

1 510-g (18-ounce) package frozen hash browns, thawed and shredded
900 g (2 pounds) sliced corned beef
230 g (8 ounces) Thousand Island salad dressing
1 425-g (15-ounce) can sauerkraut, drained
8 slices Swiss cheese

- Preheat oven to 220° C (425° F).

- Place hash browns in sprayed 23 x 33-cm (9 x 13-inch) baking dish and season with a little salt and pepper. Bake for 25 minutes.

- Place overlapping corned beef slices on top of potatoes.

- Spoon half dressing over top of beef and arrange sauerkraut over beef. Cover with slices of cheese.

- Reduce oven to 190° C (375° F) and bake for 20 minutes. Serve remaining dressing on the side. Serves 8.

Quick-Friday-Night Dinner

1 850-g (30-ounce) jar bolognaise
    sauce
2 425-g (15-ounce) cans
    borlotti beans with
    juice
800 g (28 ounces) ready-made
    spinach and ricotta
    canneloni
230 g (8 ounces) shredded
    cheddar cheese

- Preheat oven to 175° C (350° F).

- Spoon half pasta sauce
  into sprayed 23 x 33-cm
  (9 x 13-inch) baking pan and
  spread out with back of large
  spoon.

- Spread beans with juice over
  sauce. Spread canneloni over
  beans.

- Pour remaining sauce over
  canneloni. Sprinkle about ½ cup
  (60 g) cheese over top, cover
  and bake for 30 minutes.

- Remove from oven and sprinkle
  remaining cheese over top of
  canneloni.

- Return to oven for just
  5 minutes. Serves 8.

Crunchy Chicken

Spicy, Tame, Light and Full of Goodness

Crunchy Chicken Contents

Tasty Chicken with Rice and Veggies

4 skinless chicken breast halves
560 g (20 ounces) sweet-and-sour sauce
450 g (16 ounces) frozen broccoli florets, cauliflower and carrots, thawed
280 g (10 ounces) frozen baby peas, thawed
2 cups (200 g) sliced celery
1 170-g (6-ounce) package instant rice mix
⅓ cup (55 g) toasted, slivered almonds
50 g shredded parmesan cheese

- Cut chicken into 2-cm (1-inch) strips.

- Combine chicken, sweet-and-sour sauce and all vegetables in sprayed 6-L (6-quart) slow cooker.

- Cover and cook on low for 4 to 6 hours.

- When ready to serve cook rice according to package directions and fold in parmesan and almonds.

- Serve chicken and vegetables over rice. Serves 8.

A 'free-range' chicken is one that is given twice as much room as mass-produced chickens and is free to roam indoors and outdoors.

Golden Chicken Dinner

5 skinless chicken breast halves
6 medium new potatoes with peels, cubed
6 medium carrots
1 tablespoon (2 g) dried parsley flakes
1 teaspoon salt
1 280-g (10-ounce) can mushroom soup
1 280-g (10-ounce) can cream of chicken soup
¼ cup (15 g) dried mashed potato flakes

- Cut chicken into 1-cm (½-inch) pieces.
- Place potatoes and carrots in slow cooker and top with chicken.
- Sprinkle parsley flakes, salt and a little pepper over chicken.
- Combine soups in bowl and spread over chicken.
- Cover and cook on low for 6 to 7 hours.
- Stir in potato flakes and a little water or milk if necessary to make gravy and cook for additional 30 minutes. Serves 8.

King Henry IV of France was the first to state that everyone in his realm should 'have a chicken in his pot every Sunday'.

Tortellini Dinner

1 250-g (9-ounce) package
refrigerated cheese
tortellini
280 g (10 ounces) frozen green
peas, thawed
1 230-g (8-ounce) carton cream
cheese with chives
and onion
½ cup (120 g) sour cream
250 g (9 ounces) cooked
chicken breasts, cut
into strips

- Cook pasta in saucepan according to package directions.
- Place peas in colander and pour hot pasta water over green peas.
- Return pasta and peas to saucepan.
- Combine cream cheese and sour cream in smaller saucepan and heat on low, stirring well until cheese melts.
- Spoon mixture over pasta and peas and toss with heat on low.
- Heat cooked chicken in frypan or microwave.
- Spoon pasta and peas in serving bowl and place chicken on top. Serves 6.

If chicken breasts cost less than 50% more per kilogram than whole chickens, then the breasts are a better buy.

Delightful Chicken and Veggies

4–5 boneless skinless, chicken breast halves
1 425-g (15-ounce) can corn, drained
280 g (10 ounces) frozen green peas, thawed
1 455-g (16-ounce) jar alfredo pasta sauce
1 teaspoon chicken seasoning
1 teaspoon minced garlic
Pasta, cooked

- Brown chicken in frypan and place in sprayed, slow cooker.

- Combine corn, peas, alfredo sauce, ¼ cup (60 ml) water, chicken seasoning and minced garlic and pour over chicken breasts. Cover and cook on low for 4 to 5 hours. Serve over pasta. Serves 8.

Summertime Lime Chicken

6 large skinless chicken breast halves
170 ml (6 ounces) lime juice cordial
3 tablespoons (35 g) brown sugar
½ cup (135 g) chilli sauce
Rice, cooked

- Sprinkle chicken with a little salt and pepper and place in sprayed frypan. Cook on high heat and brown on both sides for about 10 minutes. Remove from frypan and keep warm.

- Add lime cordial, brown sugar and chilli sauce to frypan. Bring to a boil and cook, stirring constantly, for 4 minutes.

- Return chicken to frypan and spoon sauce over chicken. Reduce heat, cover and simmer for 15 minutes. Serve over rice. Serves 6.

Chicken Dinner Ready

4–5 carrots
6 medium new (red)
**   potatoes with peels,**
**   quartered**
4–5 skinless chicken
**   breast halves**
1 tablespoon (10 g) chicken
**   seasoning**
2 280-g (10-ounce) cans
**   cream of chicken**
**   soup**
⅓ cup (85 ml) white wine or
**   cooking wine**

- Cut carrots into 1-cm (½-inch) pieces.

- Place potatoes and carrots in slow cooker.

- Sprinkle chicken with chicken seasoning and place over vegetables.

- Spoon soup mixed with ¼ cup (60 ml) water and wine over chicken and vegetables.

- Cover and cook on low for 5 to 6 hours. Serves 5.

TIP: For a tasty change, use a can of mushroom soup instead of one can of cream of chicken soup.

The best way to tell when chicken is done is to insert a meat thermometer into the thickest parts of the chicken near the bone. The temperature should read no lower than 70° C (160° F) to be safe. Another way to tell when chicken is cooked is when the juices are clear or there is no pink colour next to the bone. If there is pink in the chicken it needs to cook a little longer.

Honey-Glazed Chicken

4 skinless chicken breast halves
Canola oil
1 625-g (22-ounce) can pineapple
  chunks with juice
½ cup (125 g) honey-mustard
  dressing
1 green capsicum, thinly
  sliced
1 red capsicum, thinly
  sliced
280 g (10 ounces) couscous,
  cooked

- Cut chicken into strips, add a little salt and pepper and brown in large frypan with a little oil.

- Add juice from pineapple, cover and simmer for 15 minutes.

- Add honey-mustard dressing, capsicum slices and pineapple chunks to chicken. Bring to a boil, reduce heat, cover and simmer for additional 15 minutes. Serve over couscous. Serves 4.

While some consider couscous a pasta because it is made from semolina and water, purists tend to consider it a separate type of food. It is grain-shaped and is sometimes mistaken for a grain. Originally from North Africa, it is increasingly popular in Australia.

Chicken-Risoni Florentine

4 skinless chicken breast halves
¾ cup (120 g) risoni
230 g (8 ounces) fresh
    mushrooms, sliced
280 g (10 ounces) frozen
    spinach, thawed and well
    drained*
1 280-g (10-ounce) can
    mushroom soup
½ cup (110 g) mayonnaise
1 tablespoon (15 ml) lemon juice
230 g (8 ounces) shredded
    cheddar cheese
½ cup (60 g) seasoned Italian
    breadcrumbs

- Preheat oven to 175° C (350° F).

- Cook chicken in boiling water
  for about 15 minutes and reserve
  stock. Cut chicken into bite-
  sized pieces and set aside. Pour
  stock through strainer and cook
  risoni in remaining stock.

- Sauté mushrooms in large,
  sprayed frypan until tender.
  Remove from heat and stir in
  chicken, risoni, spinach, soup,
  mayonnaise, lemon juice and
  ½ teaspoon pepper. Fold in half
  cheese and mix well.

- Spoon into sprayed 23 x 33-cm
  (9 x 13-inch) baking dish and
  sprinkle with remaining cheese
  and breadcrumbs. Bake for
  35 minutes. Serves 8.

*TIP: Squeeze spinach between
    paper towels to completely
    remove excess moisture.

Lemon-Almond Chicken

Asparagus, lemon juice, curry powder and almonds give a flavourful twist to an otherwise ordinary chicken dish.

2 410-g (14½-ounce) cans
    sliced asparagus,
    well-drained
4 skinless chicken
    breast halves, cut into
    1-cm (½-inch) strips
½ teaspoon chicken salt
3 tablespoons (45 g) butter
1 280-g (10-ounce) can
    cream of asparagus
    soup
⅔ cup (150 g) mayonnaise
¼ cup (60 ml) milk
1 red capsicum, cut in strips

2 tablespoons (30 ml) lemon
    juice
1 teaspoon curry powder
¼ teaspoon ground ginger
½ cup (95 g) sliced almonds,
    toasted

- Preheat oven to 175° C (350° F).

- Place asparagus in sprayed 18 x 28-cm (7 x 11-inch) baking dish and set aside. Sprinkle chicken with chicken salt.

- Sauté chicken in butter in large frypan for about 15 minutes.

- Spoon chicken over asparagus. Combine asparagus soup, mayonnaise, milk, red capsicum, lemon juice, curry powder, ginger and ¼ teaspoon pepper in frypan and heat just enough to mix well.

- Spoon over chicken and sprinkle almonds over top of casserole. Bake for 35 minutes. Serves 6.

Italian Chicken over Polenta

450 g (1 pound) chicken tenderloins, each cut in half
Canola oil
1 onion, chopped
1 425-g (15-ounce) can Italian tomatoes
⅔ cup (85 g) pitted kalamata olives
¾ cup (120 g) polenta
⅔ cup (70 g) grated parmesan cheese

- Season chicken with a little salt and pepper. Place in large frypan with a little oil.

- Add onion and cook, covered, over medium-high heat for about 8 minutes and turn once. Add tomatoes and olives, cover and cook for additional 8 minutes or until chicken is done.

- Place 2½ cups (625 ml) water in saucepan and bring to a boil. Stir in polenta and ½ teaspoon salt and cook, stirring occasionally until mixture starts to thicken.

- Stir in cheese. Spoon polenta onto serving plates and top with chicken and sauce. Serves 6.

Spicy Orange Chicken over Noodles

450 g (1 pound) boneless, skinless
   chicken tenderloins
2 tablespoons (30 ml) canola oil
2 tablespoons (30 ml) soy sauce
450 g (16 ounces)
   frozen stir-fry
   vegetables, thawed
2 cups (110 g) chow mein noodles
⅔ cup (215 g) orange marmalade
1 tablespoon (15 ml) canola oil
1 tablespoon (15 ml) soy sauce
1½ teaspoons lime juice
½ teaspoon minced ginger
½ teaspoon cayenne
   pepper

- Lightly brown chicken in oil in large frypan over medium-high heat. Add soy sauce and cook for an additional 3 minutes.

- Add stir-fry vegetables and cook for about 5 minutes or until vegetables are tender but crisp.

- Combine marmalade, oil, soy sauce, lime juice, minced ginger and cayenne pepper in saucepan and mix well.

- Heat and pour over stir-fry chicken and vegetables. Mix well and serve over noodles. Serves 6.

Creamed Chicken and Vegetables

**4 large skinless
    chicken breast halves
1 280-g (10-ounce) can cream of
    chicken soup
450 g (16 ounces) frozen
    peas and carrots, thawed
340 ml (12 ounces) chicken
    gravy**

- Cut chicken in thin slices.

- Pour soup and ½ cup (125 ml) water into sprayed 6-L (6-quart) slow cooker, mix and add chicken slices.

- Sprinkle a little salt and lots of pepper over chicken and soup. Cover and cook on low for 4 to 5 hours.

- Add peas and carrots, chicken gravy and ½ cup (125 ml) water. Increase heat to high and cook for about 1 hour or until peas and carrots are tender. Serves 6.

TIP: Serve over large dumplings or thick toast.

Do not cook with meats that are still frozen, as they may not cook thoroughly; this is not a problem with frozen vegetables.

Sunny Chicken Dinner

4 skinless chicken breast halves
1½ teaspoons curry
powder
1½ cups (375 ml) orange juice
1 tablespoon (20 g) brown sugar
1 cup (95 g) rice
1 teaspoon mustard

- Rub chicken with curry powder and a little salt and pepper. Combine orange juice, brown sugar, rice and mustard in large frypan and mix well.

- Place chicken on top of rice mixture and bring to a boil. Reduce heat, cover and simmer for 30 minutes. Remove from heat and let stand covered for about 10 minutes until all liquid absorbs into rice. Serves 4.

Roasted Chicken and Vegetables

1.4 kg (3 pounds) chicken pieces
1 cup (250 ml) Tuscan
marinade
450 g (16 ounces) frozen mixed
vegetables, thawed
¼ cup (60 ml) olive oil

- Preheat oven to 190° C (375° F).

- Arrange chicken skin-side down in sprayed baking pan. Pour ⅔ cup (150 ml) marinade over chicken.

- Bake for 30 minutes. Turn chicken over and baste with remaining ⅓ cup (75 ml) marinade.

- Toss vegetables with oil and ½ teaspoon salt. Arrange vegetables around chicken and cover with foil. Return pan to oven and bake for additional 30 minutes. Serves 8.

5ffff5ff5

ff5fffffff5fff5fff5ff5fff5ff5ff5fff5

ffffffffff4ffff4fffff4fffffffffffffffffff4

Three Cheers for Chicken

This chicken casserole is a meal in itself. Just add a tossed green salad and you have a completely, delicious, satisfying meal.

8 skinless chicken breast halves
6 tablespoons (85 g) butter
1 cup (100 g) chopped celery
1 onion, chopped
1 small green capsicum, chopped
1 115-g (4-ounce) jar chopped roasted red capsicums, drained
1 cup (95 g) rice
1 280-g (10-ounce) can cream of chicken soup
1 280-g (10-ounce) can cream of celery soup
2 soup cans milk
1 230-g (8-ounce) can sliced water chestnuts, drained
1½ cups (170 g) shredded cheddar cheese

- Preheat oven to 160° C (325° F).

- Place chicken breasts in sprayed 25 x 38-cm (10 x 15-inch) baking dish and sprinkle with a little salt and pepper.

- Melt butter in large frypan and sauté celery, onion and green capsicum. Add roasted red capsicum, rice, soups, milk and water chestnuts and mix well. Pour mixture over chicken.

- Cover and cook for 1 hour. Uncover and cook for additional 10 minutes. Remove from oven, sprinkle cheese over top of casserole and bake for additional 5 minutes. Serves 8 to 10.

Chicken-Tortilla Dumplings

This is not exactly a casserole, but it is a one-dish dinner and these dumplings are wonderful. This recipe is actually easy. It just takes a little time to add tortilla strips, one at a time. Using tortillas is certainly a lot easier than making up scone dough for the dumplings!

6 large skinless chicken breasts
2 sticks celery, chopped
1 onion, chopped
2 tablespoons (20 g) chicken stock powder
1 280-g (10-ounce) can cream of chicken soup
10 18-cm (8-inch) flour tortillas

- Place chicken, 10 cups (2.5 L) water, celery and onion in very large soup pot or roasting pan. Bring to a boil, reduce heat and cook for about 30 minutes or until chicken is tender. Remove chicken and set aside to cool.

- Save stock in roasting pan. You should have about 9 cups (2.1 L) stock. Add chicken stock and taste to make sure it is rich and tasty. If needed, add more stock. Add more water if you don't have 9 cups (2.1 L) of stock.

- When chicken is cool enough, cut into bite-size pieces and set aside. Add chicken soup to stock and bring to boil.

- Cut tortillas into 5 x 2-cm (2 x 1-inch) strips. Add strips, one at a time, to briskly boiling stock mixture and stir constantly. When all strips are in saucepan, pour in chicken, reduce heat to low and simmer for 5 to 10 minutes, stirring well but gently to prevent dumplings from sticking. Serves 10 to 12.

TIP: Your pot of chicken and dumplings will be very thick. Pour into very large serving bowl and serve hot.

Stir-Fried Chicken Spaghetti

**450 g (1 pound) skinless chicken
  breast halves**
Canola oil
**1½ cups (110 g) sliced
  mushrooms**
**1½ cups (140 g) capsicum
  strips**
**1 cup (270 g) sweet-and-sour
  stir-fry sauce**
**450 g (16 ounces) spaghetti,
  cooked**
¼ cup (60 g) butter

- Season chicken with a little salt and pepper and cut into thin slices. Brown chicken slices in large frypan with a little oil and cook for 5 minutes on medium-low heat. Transfer to plate and set aside.

- In same frypan with a little more oil, stir-fry mushrooms and capsicum strips for 5 minutes. Add chicken strips and sweet-and-sour sauce and stir until ingredients are hot.

- While pasta is still hot, drain well, add butter and stir until butter melts. Place in large bowl and toss with chicken mixture. Serve hot. Serves 8.

Stir-Fried Cashew Chicken

Canola oil
450 g (1 pound) chicken tenders,
    cut into strips
1 450-g (16-ounce) package
    frozen broccoli florets,
    cauliflower and
    carrots
1 230-g (8-ounce) jar stir-fry
    sauce
⅓ cup (45 g) cashew halves
1 340-g (12-ounce) package
    chow mein noodles

• Place a little oil and stir-fry
  chicken strips in 30-cm
  (12-inch) wok over high heat
  for about 4 minutes.

• Add vegetables and stir-fry an
  additional 4 minutes or until
  vegetables are tender. Stir in
  stir-fry sauce and cashews and
  cook just until mixture is hot.
  Serve over chow mein noodles.
  Serves 6.

Frypan Chicken and Peas

Canola oil
4–5 skinless chicken
    breast halves
2 280-g (10-ounce) cans
    cream of chicken
    soup
Paprika
2 cups (190 g) instant rice
280 g (10 ounces) frozen green
    peas

• Heat a little oil in very large
  frypan. Add chicken and cook
  until it browns well. Transfer
  chicken to plate and keep warm.

• To same frypan, add soup,
  1¾ cups (425 ml) water and
  about ½ teaspoon pepper and
  paprika. Heat to boiling, stir in
  rice and peas and reduce heat.
  Place chicken on top. Cover and
  cook on low heat for 15 minutes.
  Serves 6.

Frypan Chicken and More

4 skinless chicken breast halves
Canola oil
2 280-g (10-ounce) cans
  cream of chicken
  soup
2 cups (190 g) instant white
  rice
450 g (16 ounces) broccoli florets

- Brown chicken on both sides in very large frypan with a little oil and simmer for 10 minutes.

- Remove chicken and keep warm. Add soup and 2 cups (500 ml) water. Heat to boiling.

- Stir in rice and broccoli.

- Use a little salt, pepper and paprika on chicken and place on top of rice.

- Cover and cook on low for 15 minutes or until liquid evaporates. Serves 8.

TIP: If you have an electric frypan, it would be perfect for this dish.

Bone chicken breasts with kitchen shears for a neater job.

Seasoned Chicken over Tex-Mex Corn

2 teaspoons garlic powder
1 teaspoon ground cumin
⅔ cup (80 g) flour
4 skinless chicken breast halves
Canola oil
1 280-g (10-ounce) packet
  chicken stock
1½ cups (395 g) hot salsa
1 310-g (11-ounce) can corn
1 teaspoon Mexican seasoning
1 cup (95 g) instant rice
1 tablespoon (5 g) fresh coriander
1 tablespoon (15 ml) lemon juice

- Combine garlic powder, cumin, flour and ample salt in shallow bowl. Dip chicken in flour mixture and coat each side of chicken.

- Place a little oil in heavy frypan over medium-high heat. Cut each chicken breast in half lengthwise. Brown each piece of chicken on both sides, reduce heat and add 2 tablespoons (30 ml) water to frypan.

- Cover and simmer for 15 minutes. Transfer chicken to foil-lined baking pan and place in oven at 120° C (250° F) until Tex-Mex Corn is ready to serve.

- Using same frypan, combine stock, salsa, corn and seasoning and cook for about 10 minutes.

- Stir in rice, coriander and lemon juice and let stand for 10 minutes or until rice is tender.

- To serve, spoon Tex-Mex Corn on platter and place chicken breasts over corn. Serves 4.

Chicken Bake

**1 30-g (1-ounce) packet
vegetable soup mix**
**170 g (6 ounces) chicken
stuffing mix**
4 skinless chicken breast halves
**1 280-g (10-ounce) can cream
of mushroom soup**
⅓ cup (80 g) sour cream

- Preheat oven to 190° C (375° F).

- Toss contents of vegetable-
  seasoning packet, stuffing mix
  and 1⅔ cups (400 ml) water
  and set aside. Place chicken in
  sprayed 23 x 33-cm
  (9 x 13-inch) baking dish.

- Mix soup and sour cream in
  saucepan over low heat just
  enough to pour over chicken.
  Spoon stuffing evenly over top.
  Bake for 40 minutes. Serves 4.

Chicken Super Dinner

5 skinless chicken breast halves
5 slices onion
**5 potatoes, peeled and
quartered**
**1 280-g (10-ounce) can cream
of celery soup**

- Preheat oven to 160° C (325° F).

- Place chicken in sprayed
  23 x 33-cm (9 x 13-inch) baking
  dish. Top chicken with onion
  slices and place potatoes around
  chicken.

- Heat soup with ¼ cup (60 ml)
  water in saucepan, just enough
  to pour soup over chicken and
  vegetables. Cover and bake for
  1 hour 10 minutes. Serves 5.

Chicken Cacciatore

1 1.1-kg (2½-pound) frying
   chicken
Canola oil
2 onions, sliced
1 425-g (15-ounce) can
   tomatoes
1 230-g (8-ounce) jar tomato
   simmer sauce
1 teaspoon dried oregano
1 teaspoon celery seed

- Quarter chicken and sprinkle with plenty of salt and pepper. Place in large frypan on medium-high heat with a little oil. Add sliced onions and cook until chicken is tender (about 15 minutes).

- Combine tomatoes, simmer sauce, oregano and celery seed in saucepan. Bring mixture to a boil, reduce heat and simmer for about 20 minutes. Serves 4.

TIP: This is great over hot, cooked noodles or spaghetti.

It's no secret that tomatoes are a critical part of our cooking. They are healthy and can be turned into many wonderful sauces. There are many styles to choose from, including whole, crushed, canned, diced and sun-dried. We recommend that you keep your shelves well stocked with plenty of canned tomatoes because many recipes include them.

Chicken and the Works

6 skinless chicken breast halves
Paprika
Canola oil
2 280-g (10-ounce) cans
  cream of chicken
  soup
2 cups (190 g) instant rice
280 g (10 ounces) frozen green
  peas, thawed

- Sprinkle chicken with pepper and paprika and brown in 30-cm (12-inch) frypan with a little oil. Reduce heat, cover and simmer for about 15 minutes. Transfer chicken to plate and keep warm.

- Add soup and 2 cups (500 ml) water to frypan and mix well. Heat to boiling and stir in rice and green peas. Top with chicken breasts, cover and simmer over low heat for about 15 minutes. Serves 6.

Cheesy Swiss Chicken

4 skinless chicken breast halves
Canola oil
⅓ cup (85 ml) honey-mustard
  dressing
8 slices fully cooked bacon
4 slices Swiss cheese

- Cook chicken in large frypan with a little oil on medium-high heat for 5 minutes.

- Remove chicken to cutting board and liberally spread each breast with honey-mustard dressing.

- Top with 2 slices bacon for each breast and cover with 1 slice of Swiss cheese.

- Carefully lift each chicken breast back into frypan and place 1 tablespoon (15 ml) water in frypan. Cover and cook on medium-low heat for 10 minutes. Serves 4.

Chicken and Sauerkraut

**6 large skinless
    chicken breast halves
1 425-g (15-ounce) can sliced
    potatoes, drained
1 455-g (16-ounce) can
    sauerkraut, drained
¼ cup (30 g) pine nuts or
    ½ teaspoon caraway seeds**

- Season chicken in large frypan with a little pepper and cook over medium heat for 15 minutes or until chicken browns on both sides.

- Add potatoes to frypan and spoon sauerkraut over potatoes. Cover and cook over low heat for 35 minutes or until chicken is done.

- Toast pine nuts in dry frypan on medium heat until golden brown. Stir constantly. Sprinkle chicken and sauerkraut with toasted pine nuts or caraway seeds and serve. Serves 6.

TIP: This is good served with sour cream.

Broccoli-Cheese Chicken

1 tablespoon (15 g) butter
4 skinless chicken breast halves
200 g (7 ounces) processed
    cheese spread
350 g (12 ounces)
    frozen broccoli florets
½ cup (125 ml) milk
Rice, cooked

- Heat butter in frypan, cook chicken for 15 minutes or until brown on both sides, remove and set aside.

- In same frypan, combine cheese, broccoli, milk and a little pepper and heat to boiling. Return chicken to frypan and reduce heat to low.

- Cover and cook for additional 25 minutes until chicken is no longer pink and broccoli is tender. Serve over rice. Serves 4.

Hydrogenated oil is made from the cheapest oil-producing plants possible, usually cottonseed, corn and soybeans. Walter Willet, principal member of the Harvard Nurses' health study (the largest single controlled study in human history), suggests that hydrogenated oil is the worst food we are currently consuming.

Alfredo Chicken

**5–6 skinless chicken
   breast halves**
Canola oil
**450 g (16 ounces) frozen
   broccoli florets, thawed**
**1 red capsicum, seeded and
   chopped**
**1 450-g (16-ounce) jar alfredo
   pasta sauce**

- Preheat oven to 160° C (325° F).

- Brown and cook chicken in large frypan with a little oil until juices run clear.

- Transfer to sprayed 23 x 33-cm (9 x 13-inch) baking dish.

- Microwave broccoli according to package directions and drain. (If broccoli stems are extra long, trim and discard.)

- Spoon broccoli and capsicum over chicken.

- Heat alfredo sauce with ¼ cup (60 ml) water in small saucepan.

- Pour over chicken and vegetables. Cover and cook for 15 to 20 minutes. Serves 6.

TIP: This chicken-broccoli dish can be 'dressed up' a bit by sprinkling a little shredded parmesan cheese over the top after casserole comes out of the oven.

Savoury Chicken Fettuccini

900 g (2 pounds) boneless, skinless chicken thighs, cubed
½ teaspoon garlic powder
½ teaspoon black pepper
1 red capsicum, chopped
2 sticks celery, chopped
1 280-g (10-ounce) can cream of celery soup
1 280-g (10-ounce) can cream of chicken soup
230 g (8 ounces) cubed processed cheese
1 115-g (4-ounce) jar diced roasted red capsicums
455 g (16 ounces) spinach fettuccini

- Place chicken in slow cooker.

- Sprinkle with garlic powder, black pepper, red capsicum and celery. Top with soups.

- Cover and cook on high for 4 to 6 hours or until chicken juices are clear.

- Stir in cheese and roasted red capsicum. Cover and cook until cheese melts.

- Cook pasta according to package directions and drain.

- Place pasta in serving bowl and spoon chicken over pasta. Serve hot. Serves 10.

Imperial Chicken

1 170-g (6-ounce) box mixed
  long-grain and wild rice
2 teaspoons Oriental seasoning
1 455-g (16-ounce) jar
  garlic and parmesan
  pasta sauce
6 skinless chicken breast halves
450 g (16 ounces) frozen
  green beans, thawed
½ cup (85 g) slivered almonds,
  toasted

- Pour 2½ cups (625 g) water, rice and seasoning into sprayed slow cooker and stir well.

- Spoon in pasta sauce and mix well.

- Place chicken in slow cooker and cover with green beans.

- Cover and cook on low for 3 to 5 hours.

- When ready to serve, sprinkle with slivered almonds. Serves 6.

On average, each person eats about 80 tomatoes annually in the form of fresh, processed, chopped, stewed, ketchup, sauces, juices and hundreds of consumer products that use tomatoes.

Chicken Parmigiana and Spaghetti

1 400-g (14-ounce) package
  frozen, cooked,
  crumbed chicken
  cutlets, thawed
1 795-g (28-ounce) jar
  spaghetti sauce,
  divided
280 g (10 ounces) grated
  parmesan cheese
230 g (8 ounces) spaghetti,
  cooked

- Preheat oven to 205° C (400° F).

- Place cutlets in sprayed 23 x 33-cm (9 x 13-inch) baking dish. Top each with about ¼ cup (70 g) spaghetti sauce and 1 heaped tablespoon parmesan. Bake for 15 minutes.

- Place cooked pasta on serving platter and top with cutlets. Sprinkle remaining cheese over cutlets. Heat remaining spaghetti sauce and serve with chicken and pasta. Serves 6 to 8.

Researchers have found that tomatoes have a large amount of lycopene in them. Lycopene is a powerful antioxidant. The high vitamin, mineral and nutrient values of tomatoes may help slow down the ageing process and some degenerative diseases such as cancers, cardiovascular disease and blindness.

Hawaiian Chicken

2 small, whole chickens,
   quartered
Flour
Canola oil
1 570-g (20-ounce) can sliced
   pineapple with juice
2 green capsicums, cut in strips
Rice, cooked
1 cup (200 g) sugar
3 tablespoons (20 g) cornflour
¾ cup (175 ml) vinegar
1 tablespoon (15 ml) lemon juice
1 tablespoon (15 ml) soy sauce
2 teaspoons chicken
   stock powder

- Preheat oven to 175° C (350° F). Wash and pat chicken dry with paper towels. Shake a little salt, pepper and flour on chicken. Brown chicken in oil and place in 25 x 38-cm (10 x 15-inch) baking pan.

- Drain pineapple into 2-cup (500-ml) measuring jug. Add water (or orange juice if you have it) to make 1½ cups (375 ml) liquid. Reserve juice for sauce.

- Combine 1½ cups (375 ml) juice, sugar, cornflour, vinegar, lemon juice, soy sauce and chicken stock powder in medium saucepan.

- Bring to a boil, stir constantly until thick and clear and pour over chicken. Cover and bake for 40 minutes.

- Place pineapple slices and capsicum on top of chicken and bake for additional 10 minutes. Serve over white rice. Serves 8.

Almond-Crusted Chicken

1 egg
¼ cup (30 g) seasoned
    breadcrumbs
1 cup (170 g) slivered almonds
4 skinless chicken breast halves
145 g (5 ounces) grated
    parmesan cheese
1 teaspoon minced garlic
⅓ cup (55 g) finely chopped
    onion
2 tablespoons (30 ml) canola oil
1 cup (250 ml) white wine
¼ cup (60 ml) teriyaki sauce

- Preheat oven to 175° C (350° F).

- Place egg and 1 teaspoon water
  in shallow bowl and beat. In
  another shallow bowl, combine
  breadcrumbs and almonds.

- Dip each chicken breast in egg,
  then in almond mixture and
  place in sprayed 23 x 33-cm
  (9 x 13-inch) baking pan. Bake
  for 20 minutes.

- Remove chicken from oven and
  sprinkle parmesan cheese over
  each breast. Cook for additional
  15 minutes or until almonds and
  cheese are golden brown.

- Sauté garlic and onion in
  saucepan with oil. Add wine
  and teriyaki sauce. Bring to a
  boil, reduce heat and simmer
  for about 10 minutes or until
  mixture reduces by half.

- When serving, divide sauce
  among four plates and place
  chicken breast on top. Serves 4.

Chicken and Everything Good

**2 280-g (10-ounce) cans
  cream of chicken soup**
⅓ cup (75 g) butter, melted
**3 cups (420 g) cooked, cubed
  chicken**
**1 450-g (16-ounce) package
  frozen broccoli, corn
  and red capsicum**
**280 g (10 ounces) frozen
  green peas**
230 g (8 ounces) stuffing mix

- Combine soup, butter and ⅓ cup (85 ml) water in bowl and mix well.

- Add chicken, vegetables and stuffing mix and stir well. Spoon mixture into sprayed large slow cooker.

- Cover and cook on low for 5 to 6 hours or on high for 2 hours 30 minutes to 3 hours. Serves 8.

Use different coatings on chicken for a variety of flavours: cracker crumbs, unsweetened cereal, cornflakes, bran, half flour and half cornflour, and flour and oat bran.

Hurry-Up Chicken Enchiladas

2½–3 cups (350–420 g) cooked,
    cubed chicken breast
1 280-g (10-ounce) can
    cream of chicken
    soup
2 cups (395 g) chunky salsa
8 15-cm (6-inch) flour
    tortillas
200 g (7 ounces) processed cheese
    spread

- Combine chicken, soup and ½ cup (130 g) salsa in saucepan and heat. Spoon about ⅓ cup (70 g) chicken mixture in centre of each tortilla and roll tortilla.

- Place seam-side down in sprayed 23 x 33-cm (9 x 13-inch) baking dish. Mix cheese spread, remaining salsa and ¼ cup (60 ml) water and pour over enchiladas.

- Cover with baking paper and microwave on high, turning several times for 5 minutes or until bubbly. Serves 6.

When you need cooked chicken, boil it in water and turn off heat after it is three-quarters cooked. Cover the pot and leave chicken in the pot for about 1 hour to finish cooking. This method produces juicier and more tender chicken.

Catch-a-Chicken Casserole

3 cups (420 g) cooked, chopped
  chicken or turkey
450 g (16 ounces) frozen broccoli
  florets, thawed
1 280-g (10-ounce) can cream
  of chicken soup
⅔ cup (150 g) mayonnaise
1 cup (115 g) shredded cheddar
  cheese
1½ cups (90 g) crushed cheese
  crackers

- Preheat oven to 175° C (350° F).

- Combine chicken, broccoli,
  soup, mayonnaise and cheese
  in bowl and mix well.

- Pour into sprayed 3-L (3-quart)
  baking dish and spread cheese
  crackers over top.

- Bake for 40 minutes.
  Serves 6 to 8.

Family Chicken Casserole

1 200-g (7-ounce) packet
  chicken-flavoured
  instant rice
3 cups (420 g) cooked, chopped
  chicken or turkey
1 280-g (10-ounce) can cream
  of mushroom soup
1 280-g (10-ounce) can cream
  of celery soup
280 g (10 ounces) frozen peas,
  thawed
1 cup (115 g) shredded cheddar
  cheese

- Preheat oven to 175° C (350° F).

- Cook rice according to package
  directions.

- Combine chicken, rice, soups
  mixed with ½ cup (125 ml)
  water, peas, cheese and ½ cup
  (125 ml) water in bowl and mix
  well.

- Pour into sprayed 3-L (3-quart)
  baking dish. Cover and bake for
  40 minutes. Serves 8.

Speedy Chicken Pie

This is a 'speedy' lunch that gives you extra time to create a special dessert.

340 g (12 ounces) shredded cheddar cheese
280 g (10 ounces) frozen, chopped broccoli florets, thawed and drained
2 cups (280 g) cooked, finely diced chicken breasts
½ cup (80 g) finely chopped onion
½ cup (75 g) finely chopped red capsicum
1⅓ cups (330 ml) unthickened cream
3 eggs
¾ cup (90 g) scone mix

- Preheat oven to 175° C (350° F).

- Combine 2 cups (230 g) cheddar cheese, broccoli, chicken, onion and capsicum in bowl.

- Spread into sprayed 25-cm (10-inch) pie dish.

- In separate bowl, beat cream, eggs, scone mix, ½ teaspoon salt and ¼ teaspoon pepper and mix well.

- Slowly pour cream-egg mixture over broccoli-chicken mixture, but do not stir.

- Cover and bake for 35 minutes or until centre of pie is firm.

- Uncover and sprinkle remaining cheese over top.

- Return to oven for about 5 minutes or just until cheese melts. Serves 8.

It is best to brown chicken over medium heat.
High heat will make the outside stringy.

Encore Chicken

Canola oil
6 skinless chicken breast halves
450 g (16 ounces) thick-and-
    chunky hot salsa
1 cup (220 g) packed light
    brown sugar
1 tablespoon (15 g) Dijon-style
    mustard
Brown rice, cooked

- Preheat oven to 160° C (325° F).

- In large frypan with a little
  oil, brown chicken and place
  in sprayed 23 x 33-cm
  (9 x 13-inch) baking dish.

- Combine salsa, brown sugar,
  mustard and ½ teaspoon salt in
  bowl and pour over chicken.
  Cover and bake for 45 minutes.
  Serve over brown rice. Serves 6.

Parmesan Chicken

2 teaspoons Italian seasoning
½ cup (100 g) grated parmesan
    cheese
¼ cup (30 g) flour
¾ teaspoon garlic powder
5 skinless chicken breast halves

- Preheat oven to 190° C (375° F).

- Combine seasoning, parmesan
  cheese, flour and garlic in
  shallow bowl.

- Moisten chicken with a little
  water and coat with cheese
  mixture. Place in sprayed
  23 x 33-cm (9 x 13-inch)
  baking pan.

- Bake for 25 minutes or until
  chicken is light brown and
  cooked thoroughly. Serves 6.

Comfort Chicken Plus

170 g (6 ounces) chicken stuffing mix
1 bunch fresh broccolini
2 sticks celery, sliced
1 cup (150 g) chopped red capsicum
2 tablespoons (30 g) butter
1 230-g (8-ounce) can corn, drained
2½ cups (350 g) finely chopped chicken or turkey
250 ml (8½ ounces) hollandaise sauce
85 g (3 ounces) onions, finely chopped and fried until crispy

- Preheat oven to 160° C (325° F).

- Prepare chicken stuffing mix according to package directions.

- Place broccolini, celery, capsicum, butter and ¼ cup (60 ml) water in microwave-safe bowl. Cover with baking paper and microwave on high for 1½ minutes.

- Add broccoli-celery mixture, corn and chicken to stuffing and mix well. Spoon into sprayed 18 x 28-cm (7 x 11-inch) baking dish.

- Mix hollandaise sauce with ¼ cup (65 ml) water. Pour sauce over casserole and sprinkle top with fried onions.

- Bake for 25 minutes. Serves 8.

It's best to put crunchy foods like celery in soups or stews towards the end of the cooking time so they will stay crunchy.

Tasty Frypan Chicken

5 large skinless
   chicken breast halves
Canola oil
1 green capsicum,
   seeded and thinly sliced
1 red capsicum, seeded and
   thinly sliced
2 small yellow squash, seeds
   removed, thinly sliced
450 g (16 ounces)
   thick-and-chunky salsa
500 g (18 ounces) instant rice,
   cooked

- Cut chicken into thin strips.
  With a little oil in large frypan,
  sauté chicken for about
  5 minutes.

- Add capsicums and squash and
  cook for an additional 5 minutes
  or until capsicum is tender but
  crisp.

- Stir in salsa and bring to a boil.
  Lower heat and simmer for
  10 minutes. Serve over rice.
  Serves 8.

To make green capsicum strips or slices, hold the capsicum upright on a cutting surface. Slice each of the sides from the stem and discard stem, white membrane and seeds.

Creamy Chicken Bake

1 230-g (8-ounce) package
    fettuccini (egg noodles)
450 g (16 ounces) frozen
    broccoli florets, thawed
¼ cup (60 g) butter, melted
230 g (8 ounces) shredded
    cheddar cheese
1 280-g (10-ounce) can cream of
    chicken soup
1 cup (250 ml) unthickened
    cream
¼ teaspoon ground mustard
3 cups (420 g) cooked, cubed
    chicken breasts
⅔ cup (110 g) slivered almonds,
    toasted

- Preheat oven to 175° C (350° F).

- Cook pasta according to package directions and drain. Combine pasta and broccoli in large bowl.

- Add butter and cheese and stir until cheese melts. Stir in chicken soup, cream, mustard, chicken and about ½ teaspoon each of salt and pepper. Spoon into sprayed 2.5-L (2½-quart) baking dish.

- Cover and bake for about 40 minutes. Remove from oven and sprinkle with slivered almonds. Serves 8.

Chicken Supreme

This dish is really delicious and so-o-o-o easy. It's a meal in itself!

1 onion, chopped
1 cup (100 g) sliced celery
3 tablespoons (45 g) butter
4 cups (560 g) cooked, diced
  chicken breast
1 170-g (6-ounce) package
  mixed long-grain and wild
  rice, cooked
1 280-g (10-ounce) can cream
  of celery soup
1 280-g (10-ounce) can
  cream of chicken soup
1 115-g (4-ounce) jar
  roasted red capsicums
2 425-g (15-ounce) cans green
  beans, drained
1 cup (170 g) slivered
  almonds
1 cup (225 g) mayonnaise
1 teaspoon white pepper
2½ cups (140 g) crushed
  potato chips

• Preheat oven to 175° C (350° F).

• Sauté onion and celery in butter in saucepan. In very large saucepan, combine onion-celery mixture, chicken, rice, soups, roasted red capsicums, green beans, almonds, mayonnaise, ½ teaspoon each of salt and white pepper and mix well.

• Spoon into sprayed 25 x 38-cm (10 x 15-inch) deep baking dish. Sprinkle crushed potato chips over top of casserole. Bake for 40 minutes or until potato chips are light brown. Serves 14.

TIP: This recipe is a great way to serve a lot of people. It will serve at least 14 to 15. It may also be made with green peas instead of green beans. If you want to make it in advance and freeze or just refrigerate for the next day, wait until you are ready to cook the casserole before adding potato chips.

Divine Chicken Casserole

750 g (26 ounces) frozen broccoli florets, thawed
1 teaspoon chicken salt
3 cups (420 g) cooked, diced chicken
1 280-g (10-ounce) can cream of chicken soup
2 tablespoons (30 ml) milk
½ cup (110 g) mayonnaise
2 teaspoons lemon juice
½ teaspoon white pepper
1 cup (115 g) shredded cheddar cheese
1½ cups (90 g) round buttery cracker crumbs
3 tablespoons (45 g) butter, melted

- Preheat oven to 175° C (350° F).

- Cook broccoli according to package directions and drain.

- Place broccoli in sprayed 23 x 33-cm (9 x 13-inch) baking dish and sprinkle chicken salt over broccoli. Cover with diced chicken.

- Combine soup, milk, mayonnaise, lemon juice, white pepper and cheese in saucepan and heat just enough to be able to pour mixture over broccoli and chicken.

- Combine cracker crumbs and butter in bowl and sprinkle over casserole. Bake for 35 to 40 minutes or until hot and bubbly. Serves 8.

Family Night Spaghetti

6 frozen crumbed, cooked
  chicken breast halves
230 g (8 ounces)
  spaghetti, cooked
1 400-g (14-ounce) jar spaghetti
  sauce
340 g (12 ounces) shredded
  mozzarella cheese

- Bake chicken according to
  package directions and keep
  warm. Cook pasta according to
  package directions, drain and
  arrange on platter.

- Place spaghetti sauce in
  saucepan with 1 cup (115 g)
  mozzarella cheese and heat
  slightly, but do not boil.

- Spoon about half sauce over
  pasta and arrange chicken
  breasts over top. Spoon
  remaining spaghetti sauce on
  chicken and sprinkle remaining
  cheese over top. Serves 6.

Frypan Chicken and Stuffing

1 170-g (6-ounce) box stuffing
  mix for chicken with
  seasoning packet
450 g (16 ounces) frozen
  corn
¼ cup (60 g) butter
4 skinless chicken breast
  halves, cooked

- Combine seasoning packet from
  stuffing mix, corn, 1⅔ cups
  (400 ml) water and butter in
  large frypan and bring to a boil.
  Reduce heat, cover and simmer
  for 5 minutes.

- Stir in stuffing mix just until
  moist. Cut chicken into thin
  slices and mix with stuffing-corn
  mixture. Cook on low heat
  just until mixture heats well.
  Serves 6.

Easy Chicken and Dumplings

3 cups (420 g) cooked,
    chopped chicken
2 280-g (10-ounce) cans
    cream of chicken
    soup
3 teaspoons chicken
    stock powder
150 g (5 ounces)
    scone mix

- Combine chopped chicken, both cans of soup, chicken stock powder and 4½ cups (1.1 L) water in large, heavy pan. Boil mixture and stir to mix well.

- Prepare scone mix according to packet directions. Drop teaspoonfuls of dough into boiling chicken mixture and stir gently.

- When all scones are dropped, reduce heat to low and simmer, stirring occasionally for about 15 minutes. Serves 8.

TIP: Deli turkey will also work in this recipe. It's a great time-saver!

Use mayonnaise (not low-fat) to get a crispy, golden brown exterior on chicken by rubbing it all over the outside before roasting.

Family Chicken Bake

This is a good, basic 'meat-and-potatoes' dish all families will love.

¼ cup (60 g) butter
1 red capsicum,
    seeded and chopped
1 onion, chopped
2 sticks celery, chopped
230 g (8 ounces)
    sour cream
1½ cups (375 ml)
    unthickened cream
200 g (7 ounces) chopped
    green chillies
1 teaspoon chicken
    stock powder
½ teaspoon celery salt
3–4 cups (420–560 g) cooked,
    cubed chicken
450 g (16 ounces) shredded
    cheddar cheese
1 900-g (2-pound) package
    frozen hash browns,
    thawed and shredded

- Preheat oven to 175° C (350° F).

- Melt butter in saucepan and sauté capsicum, onion and celery.

- Combine sour cream, cream, green chillies, stock powder, celery salt and about ½ teaspoon each of salt and pepper in large bowl.

- Stir in capsicum mixture, chicken and half of cheese. Fold in hash browns. Spoon into sprayed 25 x 38-cm (10 x 15-inch) baking dish.

- Bake for 45 minutes or until casserole is bubbly. Remove from oven and sprinkle remaining cheese over top of casserole. Return to oven for about 5 minutes. Serves 10.

TIP: For a change of pace, heat some hot, thick-and-chunky salsa to spoon over top of each serving.

Chicken Pot Pie

1 425-g (15-ounce) package
   refrigerated shortcrust
   pastry
1 540-g (19-ounce) can cream
   of chicken soup
2 cups (280 g) cooked, diced
   chicken breast
1 280-g (10-ounce) package
   frozen mixed
   vegetables, thawed

* Preheat oven to 160° C (325° F).

* Cut pastry to fit 23-cm
  (9-inch) pie pan. Line pan with
  pastry and fill with chicken
  soup, chicken and mixed
  vegetables.

* Cover with a second layer of
  pastry; trim, fold edges under
  and crimp. With knife, cut 4 slits
  in centre of pastry.

* Bake for 1 hour 15 minutes or
  until crust is golden. Serves 6.

TIP: *When you're too busy to cook
     a chicken, get a roast chicken
     from the supermarket.*

Chicken and Broccoli Casserole

3 cups (420 g) cooked, cubed
   chicken
450 g (16 ounces) frozen
   broccoli florets
230 g (8 ounces) cubed
   processed cheese
⅔ cup (150 g) mayonnaise

* Combine chicken, broccoli,
  cheese and ¼ cup (60 ml) water
  in frypan. Cover and cook over
  medium heat until broccoli is
  tender but crisp and cheese
  melts. Stir in mayonnaise and
  heat through, but do not boil.
  Serves 6.

TIP: *This is great served over hot,
     cooked rice.*

Chicken and Broccoli Bake

**2 100-g (3½-ounce) packets
   boil-in-the-bag rice
230 g (8 ounces) cubed
   processed cheese
450 g (16 ounces) frozen broccoli
   florets, thawed
3 cups (420 g) cooked, cubed
   chicken
1 cup cracker crumbs (60 g)
   or seasoned
   breadcrumbs (120 g)**

- Preheat oven to 160° C (325° F).

- Cook rice in large saucepan
  according to package directions.
  Stir in cheese and ¼ cup (60 ml)
  water. Stir and mix until
  cheese melts.

- Cook broccoli according to
  package directions. Add
  broccoli and chicken to rice-
  cheese mixture and mix well.

- Spoon into sprayed 23 x 33-cm
  (9 x 13-inch) baking dish.
  Top with cracker or seasoned
  breadcrumbs and bake for
  15 minutes. Serves 8.

*TIP: Just use deli chicken or turkey
      if you don't want to cook your
      own.*

Turkey Tenders with Honey-Ginger Glaze

Canola oil
Lemon pepper
450 g (1 pound) turkey tenders
Rice, cooked
⅔ cup (230 g) honey
2 teaspoons peeled,
    grated fresh ginger
1 tablespoon (15 ml)
    Worcestershire sauce
1 tablespoon (15 ml) soy sauce
Lemon juice

- Place a little oil in heavy frypan. Sprinkle lemon pepper on turkey tenders and cook for about 5 minutes on each side or until brown.

- Combine honey, ginger, Worcestershire sauce, soy sauce and lemon juice into a bowl, mix well and pour into frypan with turkey tenders.

- Bring mixture to a boil, reduce heat and simmer for 15 minutes. Serve over rice. Serves 6.

If you have a frozen turkey, allow 2 to 3 days for it to thaw in a refrigerator. It's best to let the thawed turkey sit at room temperature for about 1 hour before cooking it.

Lemon-Honey Glazed Chicken

1 1.1–1.4-kg (2½–3-pound)
  chicken, quartered
⅓ cup (115 g) honey
2 tablespoons (30 ml) lemon juice
1 30-g (1-ounce) packet onion
  soup mix

- Preheat oven to 190° C (375° F).

- Place chicken quarters, skin-side down, in sprayed 23 x 33-cm (9 x 13-inch) baking pan.

- Bake for 30 minutes. Remove from oven and turn chicken quarters over.

- Combine honey, lemon juice and onion soup mix in small bowl and brush glaze over chicken. Cook for additional 20 minutes. Brush glaze over chicken every 5 minutes. Serves 4.

Glazed Chicken and Rice

4 skinless chicken breast halves,
  cubed
1 570-g (20-ounce) can pineapple
  chunks with juice
½ cup (125 g) honey
1 teaspoon Dijon mustard
1 red capsicum, seeded, chopped
Rice, cooked

- Brown chicken in frypan with a little oil and cook on low heat for 15 minutes.

- Add pineapple, honey, mustard and capsicum and bring to a boil.

- Reduce heat to low and simmer for 10 to 15 minutes or until sauce thickens slightly.

- Serve over rice. Serves 4.

Frypan Roasted Chicken

1 1.1–1.4-kg (2½–3-pound) chicken, quartered
2 teaspoons sage
Canola oil
2 teaspoons minced garlic
2 280-g (10-ounce) cans cream of chicken soup
Rice, cooked

- Dry chicken quarters with paper towels. Sprinkle with sage and a little salt and pepper.

- Place in large frypan with a little oil. Cook on both sides over medium-high heat for about 15 minutes.

- Combine garlic, chicken soup and ½ cup (125 ml) water in saucepan. Heat just enough to blend ingredients.

- Pour over chicken, cover and cook on low heat for 5 minutes or until chicken heats thoroughly. Serve over rice. Serves 4.

Allow about ¾ cup stuffing or dressing per
500 grams of chicken when stuffing a chicken.

Honey-Roasted Chicken

3 tablespoons (45 ml) soy sauce
3 tablespoons (50 g) honey
2½ cups (80 g) crushed Weet Bix
½ cup (65 g) very finely minced
  walnuts
5–6 skinless chicken breast halves

• Preheat oven to 205° C (400° F).

• Combine soy sauce and honey
  in shallow bowl and set aside. In
  another shallow bowl, combine
  crushed Weet Bix and walnuts.

• Dip both sides of each chicken
  breast in soy sauce-honey
  mixture and dredge in cereal-
  walnut mixture.

• Place each piece on sprayed
  foil-lined baking tray. Bake for
  25 minutes (about 35 minutes if
  breasts are very large). Serves 6.

Italian Crumbed Chicken

5–6 skinless chicken
  breast halves
¾ cup (170 g) mayonnaise
⅓ cup (35 g) grated parmesan
  cheese
½ cup (60 g) Italian-seasoned
  breadcrumbs

• Preheat oven to 205° C (400° F).

• Place all chicken in foil-
  lined baking pan. Combine
  mayonnaise, 1 teaspoon pepper
  and parmesan cheese in bowl
  and mix well.

• Spread mixture over chicken
  breasts and sprinkle seasoned
  breadcrumbs on both sides.

• Bake for 20 to 25 minutes or
  until chicken is light brown.
  Breasts may be served whole or
  sliced diagonally. Serves 6.

Barbecued Chicken with Raspberry Barbecue Sauce

1 1.1-kg (2½-pound) chicken, quartered
Seasoned salt
Seasoned pepper
340 g (12 ounces) seedless raspberry jam
½ cup (85 g) barbecue sauce
2 tablespoons (30 ml) raspberry vinegar
2 tablespoons (30 g) Dijon-style mustard

- Season chicken quarters liberally with seasoned salt and pepper. Barbecue chicken, covered with barbecue lid, over medium-high heat for about 8 minutes on each side.

- While chicken cooks, combine jam, barbecue sauce, vinegar and mustard into a bowl.

- Baste chicken with sauce during last 2 minutes of cooking. Serves 4.

You can estimate about 100 to 150 grams (¼ to ⅓ pound) boneless chicken for an individual serving. A 500-gram (1 pound) packet of boneless, skinless chicken breast will yield about 2 cups cooked meat. When you buy a whole chicken, allow 1 cup cooked chicken for each 500 grams of whole chicken.

Brown Rice Chicken

300 g (11 ounces) cooked,
    chopped chicken breasts
2 250-g (8½-ounce) packages
    instant brown rice, cooked
⅔ cup (35 g) sun-dried
    tomatoes
2 ripe avocados,
    peeled and diced
¾ cup (175 ml) Dijon-style
    mustard vinaigrette
    dressing

- Combine chicken, rice, tomatoes and avocado in bowl.

- In separate bowl, combine vinaigrette dressing and ½ teaspoon salt.

- Gently stir into chicken-rice mixture and refrigerate for 2 hours before serving. Serves 6.

TIP: Instant rice goes in the microwave and is ready in 90 seconds. Not bad for the rush hour!

Sweet and Spicy Chicken Thighs

3 teaspoons chilli
  powder
3 tablespoons (50 g) honey
2 tablespoons (30 ml) lemon juice
10–12 chicken thighs

- Preheat oven to 220° C (425° F).

- Line 25 x 38-cm (10 x 15-inch) shallow baking pan with heavy foil and set metal rack in pan.

- Combine chilli powder, honey, lemon juice and lots of salt and pepper in bowl.

- Brush mixture over chicken thighs and place on rack in baking pan. Turn thighs to coat completely.

- Bake, turning once, for about 35 minutes. Serves 5 to 6.

Spanish Rice

1 230-g (8-ounce) package
  Spanish rice mix
170 g (6 ounces) chicken
  breast strips
1 310-g (11-ounce) can
  corn
60 g (2 ounces) chopped
  black olives

- Combine Spanish rice mix and 2¼ cups (560 ml) water in soup pot or large saucepan. Heat to boiling, reduce heat and cook slowly for 5 minutes.

- Add chopped chicken, corn and black olives. Heat to boiling, reduce heat and simmer for about 20 minutes. Serves 4.

TIP: You could also add leftover ham or salami and 1 tablespoon (15 ml) lemon juice to mix it up a little.

Chicken and Noodles

1 85-g (3-ounce) package
   chicken-flavoured
   instant ramen noodles
1 450-g (16-ounce) package
   frozen broccoli,
   cauliflower and carrots
⅔ cup (180 g) sweet-and-sour
   sauce
3 skinless chicken breast halves,
   cooked

- Cook noodles and vegetables in saucepan with 2 cups (500 ml) boiling water for 3 minutes, stirring occasionally, and drain.

- Combine noodle-vegetable mixture with seasoning packet, sweet-and-sour sauce and a little salt and pepper. Cut chicken into strips, add chicken to noodle mixture and heat thoroughly. Serves 6.

TIP: You may want to add 1 tablespoon (15 ml) soy sauce, if you have it on hand.

When you wash lettuce and greens for a salad, be sure to dry the leaves between paper towels. Dressing will be watered down if water is left on the leaves.

Favourite Oven-Fried Chicken

2 cups (500 ml) buttermilk
2 tablespoons (30 g) Dijon-style mustard
2 teaspoons garlic powder
1 teaspoon cayenne pepper
6 boneless, skinless chicken breast halves
2½ cups (70 g) crushed cornflakes
¾ cup (45 g) breadcrumbs
2 tablespoons (30 ml) olive oil

- Combine buttermilk, mustard, garlic powder and pepper into a large bowl and mix well. Place chicken pieces in bowl and turn to coat well. Place in refrigerator and marinate for 2 hours or overnight.

- When ready to bake, preheat oven to 205° C (400° F).

- Line large baking pan with foil and spray with cooking oil.

- Combine crushed cornflakes and breadcrumbs in large shallow bowl. Drizzle oil over crumbs and toss until they coat well.

- Take 1 piece chicken at a time, remove from marinade and dredge in crumb mixture. Press crumbs onto all sides of chicken and place in baking pan. Do not let sides touch. Bake for 35 to 40 minutes. Serves 6.

TIP: The easiest way to crush cornflakes is in a sealed plastic bag with the palm of your hand. You don't even have to get out the rolling pin if you don't want to or don't have one. Who needs a rolling pin anyway?

Super Chicken Spaghetti

This recipe is a different twist on the always-popular chicken spaghetti. This is a wonderful casserole to serve to family or for guests. It has great flavour with chicken, pasta and colourful vegetables all in one dish. It's a winner, I promise!

**1 bunch spring onions
    with tops, chopped
1 cup (100 g) chopped celery
1 red capsicum, chopped
1 yellow or orange capsicum,
    seeded and chopped
¼ cup (60 g) butter
1 tablespoon (2 g) dried
    coriander leaves
1 teaspoon Italian seasoning
230 g (8 ounces) thin
    spaghetti, cooked
    and drained
4 cups (560 g) cooked, chopped
    chicken or turkey
230 g (8 ounces) sour cream
1 455-g (16-ounce) jar creamy
    alfredo sauce**

**280 g (10 ounces) frozen
    green peas, thawed
230 g (8 ounces) shredded
    mozzarella cheese**

- Preheat oven to 175° C (350° F).

- Sauté onions, celery and capsicums in butter in large frypan. Combine onion-capsicum mixture, coriander, Italian seasoning, pasta, chicken, sour cream and alfredo sauce in large bowl and mix well.

- Sprinkle a little salt and pepper into mixture. Fold in peas and half mozzarella cheese. Spoon into sprayed 25 x 38-cm (10 x 15-inch) deep baking dish. Cover and bake for 45 minutes. Remove from oven and sprinkle remaining cheese over casserole. Return to oven for about 5 minutes. Serves 10.

Quails with Ginger-Orange Glaze

1 cup (250 ml) fresh orange juice
2 tablespoons (20 g) peeled,
**　　minced fresh ginger**
1 tablespoon (15 ml) soy sauce
3 tablespoons (50 g) honey
4 quails, halved
½ teaspoon ground
**　　ginger**

- Preheat oven to 230° C (450° F).

- Combine orange juice, ginger, soy sauce and honey in saucepan and cook on high heat, stirring constantly for 3 minutes or until thick and glossy.

- Place quails in sprayed baking dish and sprinkle ground ginger and ½ teaspoon each of salt and pepper over birds.

- Spoon glaze mixture over quails and bake for 15–20 minutes, or until juices run clear. Brush glaze over quails several times during cooking. Serves 4.

Spinach and other leafy greens are loaded with lutein, a phytochemical that travels through the bloodstream to the eye. Lutein seems to absorb the type of light that can cause macular degeneration and may help prevent cataracts. High levels of lutein in the bloodstream may help prevent fatty deposits from clogging arteries, as well.

Chicken Cassoulet

This is a great recipe for leftover chicken.

230 g (½ pound) chicken
  sausages
2 cups (280 g) cooked, cubed
  chicken
3 carrots, sliced
1 onion, halved, sliced
1 425-g (15-ounce) can
  cannellini beans
1 425-g (15-ounce) can butter
  beans
1 230-g (8-ounce) jar tomato
  simmer sauce
1 teaspoon dried thyme
¼ teaspoon ground
  allspice

• Cut sausages into 1-cm (½-inch)
  pieces. Combine all ingredients
  in sprayed slow cooker.
  Cover and cook on low for
  4 to 5 hours. Serves 6.

Turkey and Rice Olé

This may be served as a one-dish meal or as a sandwich wrap in flour tortillas.

450 g (1 pound) minced turkey
1 155-g (5½-ounce) package
  Spanish rice mix
1 425-g (15-ounce) can borlotti
  beans, rinsed and drained
1 cup (265 g) thick-and-chunky
  salsa

• Brown turkey in large frypan
  and break up large pieces with
  fork. Add rice mix and 2 cups
  (500 ml) water.

• Bring to a boil, reduce heat and
  simmer for about 8 minutes or
  until rice is tender. Stir in beans
  and salsa and cook just until
  mixture heats through. Serves 6.

Turkey and Ham Tetrazzini

This is another old-fashioned dish modified for today's 'hurry-up meal', but it keeps the same great taste.

½ cup (85 g) slivered almonds, toasted
1 280-g (10-ounce) can cream of mushroom soup
1 280-g (10-ounce) can cream of chicken soup
¾ cup (175 ml) milk
2 tablespoons (30 ml) dry white wine
230 g (8 ounces) thin spaghetti, cooked and drained
2½ cups (350 g) cooked, diced turkey
2 cups (280 g) cooked, diced ham
½ cup (75 g) chopped green capsicum
½ cup (75 g) chopped red capsicum
½ cup (65 g) halved, pitted black olives
230 g (8 ounces) shredded cheddar cheese

- Preheat oven to 175° C (350° F).

- Mix almonds, soups, milk and wine in large bowl. Stir in pasta, turkey, ham, capsicums and olives. Spoon into sprayed 23 x 33-cm (9 x 13-inch) baking dish.

- Cover and bake for 35 minutes or until casserole is hot and bubbly. Uncover and sprinkle top of casserole with cheese. Return to oven for 5 minutes. Serves 6 to 8.

Turkey-Asparagus Alfredo

1 bunch fresh asparagus
1 red capsicum, seeded, thinly sliced
230 g (½ pound) deli turkey
1 450-g (16-ounce) jar alfredo sauce
Rice, cooked

- Bring ½ cup (125 ml) water in frypan to a boil. Cut off woody ends of asparagus and cut into thirds.

- Add asparagus and capsicums and cook on medium-high heat for 4 minutes or until tender but crisp and drain.

- Slice turkey into thin strips. With frypan still on medium-high heat, stir in alfredo sauce and turkey strips.

- Bring to a boil, reduce heat and simmer until mixture heats thoroughly. Serve over rice. Serves 4.

Pears in the supermarket are usually green and hard because they ripen off the tree. The best way for them to ripen is stored in a paper bag at room temperature until the flesh at the neck gives a little when you press against it. Once ripe they should be stored in the coldest part of the refrigerator.

Cajun Turkey

Turkey tenderloins are wonderful.
You'll be glad you cooked them!

2 tablespoons (20 g) Cajun
seasoning
680–900 g (1½–2 pounds) turkey
tenderloins
1 tablespoon (5 g) fresh
chopped rosemary
1½ cups (400 g) barbecue sauce
Potatoes, mashed

- Rub seasoning evenly over turkey, sprinkle on rosemary and press into tenderloins. Cover and refrigerate for 1 to 2 hours.

- Barbecue turkey with lid closed over medium-high heat for 5 to 10 minutes on each side. Baste with half barbecue sauce.

- Let turkey stand for 10 minutes before slicing and serve with remaining barbecue sauce. Serve over mashed potatoes. Serves 6.

If you need a large turkey, consider buying two smaller
turkeys instead of one large one. It doubles the number of legs,
breasts, thighs and giblets, and you have a shorter cooking time.

Turkey Pasta

**85 g (3 ounces) two-minute
  noodles**
**1 tablespoon (10 g)
  garlic and parsley
  seasoning**
¾ cup (170 g) mayonnaise
1 cup (250 ml) milk
**3 cups (420 g) cooked, diced
  turkey**
**280 g (10 ounces)
  frozen peas**
**1 115-g (4-ounce) jar chopped
  green chillies**
¾ cup (45 g) cracker crumbs

- Preheat oven to 175° C (350° F).

- Cook noodles according to
  package directions. Drain.

- Combine seasoning, mayonnaise
  and milk in large bowl. Add
  turkey, peas and green chillies
  and mix well.

- Add noodles to turkey mixture;
  toss. Pour into sprayed 3-L
  (3-quart) baking dish.

- Cover and bake for 25 minutes.
  Uncover and sprinkle cracker
  crumbs over top of casserole.
  Return to oven for additional
  10 to 15 minutes. Serves 5 to 6.

Perfect Pork

Dipped, Smothered, Noodled and Chopped

Perfect Pork Contents

Pork Tenderloin with Cranberry Sauce

2 450-g (1-pound) pork
    tenderloins
½ cup (10 g) chopped fresh
    coriander
½ teaspoon ground
    cumin
2 teaspoons (10 ml) minced
    garlic
1 455-g (16-ounce) can whole
    cranberries
1 cup (320 g) orange marmalade
1 170-g (8-ounce) can crushed
    pineapple, drained
¾ cup (85 g) chopped pecans

- Preheat oven to 190° C (375° F).

- Season pork with a little salt and pepper, coriander, cumin and garlic.

- Place in foil-lined baking pan and bake for 15 minutes. Reduce heat to 160° C (325° F) and bake for additional 35 minutes. Slice to serve.

- Combine cranberries, marmalade, pineapple and pecans in bowl and serve with tenderloin. Sauce may be served at room temperature or warmed. Serves 8.

Grilled Pork Tenderloin with Rice and Beans

2 450-g (1-pound) pork
   tenderloins
1 tablespoon (15 ml) canola
   oil
2 tablespoons (20 g) Cajun
   seasoning
1 170-g (6-ounce) package
   chicken-flavoured rice
1 425-g (15-ounce) can borlotti
   beans, rinsed
½ cup (70 g) roasted red
   capsicum, sliced
2 tablespoons (2 g) chopped
   coriander

- Rub pork with oil and sprinkle with seasoning.

- Grill over medium-high heat for about 25 minutes, brown on both sides and cook until meat thermometer inserted in centre registers 70° C (160° F).

- Cook rice according to package directions and add beans, capsicum, coriander and a little salt and pepper.

- Spoon on serving platter.

- Slice tenderloin and arrange on top of rice-bean mixture. Serves 8.

It is best for cooked pork to have an internal temperature of 65 to 70° C (150 to 160° F) to yield the juiciest and most tender meat. Higher internal temperatures lead to dry, overcooked pork. The best way to check if pork is ready is to use a meat thermometer.

Fiesta Pork Casserole

This zesty casserole is easy to put together, and it really gets your attention! It is an especially nice change of pace from the usual Mexican dish with ground beef.

900 g (2 pounds) boneless pork tenderloin, cut into 2-cm (1-inch) cubes
1 onion, chopped
1 green capsicum, seeded and chopped
3 tablespoons (45 ml) canola oil
1 425-g (15-ounce) can borlotti beans, rinsed and drained
200 g (7 ounces) processed cheese spread
1 425-g (15-ounce) can tomatoes
1 115-g (4-ounce) jar chopped green chillies
1 cup (195 g) instant brown rice, cooked
1¼ cups (330 g) salsa

2 teaspoons ground cumin
½ teaspoon garlic powder
¾ cup (85 g) shredded cheddar cheese

- Preheat oven to 175° C (350° F).

- Brown and cook pork, onion and capsicum in oil in very large frypan until pork is no longer pink. Drain.

- Add beans, processed cheese, tomatoes, green chillies, rice, salsa, cumin, ½ teaspoon salt and garlic powder to frypan. Cook on medium heat, stirring occasionally, until mixture bubbles.

- Spoon into sprayed 4-L (4-quart) baking dish. Bake for 30 minutes or until bubbly around edges. Remove from oven and sprinkle with cheese. Let stand a few minutes before serving. Serves 8 to 10.

One-Dish Pork and Peas

So many of our casseroles are chicken, but pork is so good and always tender. This blend of ingredients makes a delicious dish.

680 g (1½ pounds) pork
   tenderloin, cut into
   1-cm (½-inch) cubes
2 tablespoons (30 ml) canola oil
1 cup (100 g) sliced celery
1 onion, chopped
1 red capsicum, seeded, chopped
230 g (8 ounces)
   linguine (egg noodles),
   cooked and drained
1 280-g (10-ounce) can cream
   of chicken soup
½ cup (125 ml) unthickened
   cream
280 g (10 ounces) frozen green
   peas, thawed
1 cup (120 g) seasoned
   breadcrumbs
⅓ cup (130 g) chopped walnuts

- Preheat oven to 175° C (350° F).

- Brown cubed pork in oil in large frypan. Reduce heat and cook for about 20 minutes. Remove pork to separate dish.

- In remaining oil, sauté celery, onion and capsicum. Add pork, pasta, soup, cream, peas, 1 teaspoon salt and ½ teaspoon pepper.

- Spoon into sprayed 3-L (3-quart) baking dish. Sprinkle with breadcrumbs and walnuts.

- Bake for about 25 minutes or until bubbly. Serves 8.

Pork and Pasta Supreme

2 tablespoons (30 ml) canola oil
900 g (2 pounds) pork
    tenderloin, cut
    into 2-cm (1-inch) cubes
2 sticks celery, chopped
1 red capsicum,
    seeded and chopped
1 green capsicum,
    seeded and chopped
1 onion, chopped
340 g (12 ounces) fettuccini
    (egg noodles), cooked
    and drained
1 280-g (10-ounce) can cream
    of celery soup
1 280-g (10-ounce) can cream
    of chicken soup
1 425-g (15-ounce) can
    creamed corn
¾ cup (185 ml) unthickened
    cream
1½ cups (45 g) crushed
    cornflakes
3 tablespoons (45 g) butter,
    melted

- Preheat oven to 175° C (350° F).

- Heat oil in frypan and brown and cook pork for about 15 minutes. Place pork into large bowl.

- With remaining oil in frypan, sauté celery, capsicums and onion. Spoon into bowl with pork. Add pasta, both soups, creamed corn, cream and ½ teaspoon each salt and pepper to pork.

- Mix well and pour into sprayed 23 x 33-cm (9 x 13-inch) baking dish.

- Combine crushed cornflakes and butter in bowl and sprinkle over casserole. Cover and bake for about 30 minutes. Serves 8.

TIP: If it's hard to find a 680-g (1½-pound) pork roast, buy 2 340-g (¾-pound) pork tenderloins. It is a little more expensive, but well worth it because you are not buying bones and the tenderloin will be tender and delicious.

Oodles of Noodles

680–900 g (1½–2 pounds) pork
    tenderloin, cut into 2-cm
    (1-inch) cubes
3 tablespoons (45 ml) canola oil
2 cups (200 g) chopped celery
1 red capsicum, seeded and
    chopped
1 green capsicum, seeded and
    chopped
1 onion, chopped
1 115-g (4-ounce) jar sliced
    mushrooms
1 280-g (10-ounce) can tomatoes
60 g (2 ounces) green chillies,
    sliced
1 teaspoon minced garlic
1 280-g (10-ounce) can cream
    of mushroom soup
1 280-g (10-ounce) can cream
    of celery soup
¼ cup (60 ml) soy sauce
230 g (8 ounces) elbow macaroni,
    cooked and drained
2 cups (110 g) chow mein noodles

- Preheat oven to 175° C (350° F).

- Brown pork in oil in frypan and cook on low heat for about 15 minutes. Remove pork with slotted spoon to side dish.

- Sauté celery, capsicums and onion in same frypan in remaining oil. Combine pork, celery-onion mixture, mushrooms, tomatoes, green chillies, garlic, soups, soy sauce and pasta in large bowl.

- Spoon into sprayed 23 x 33-cm (9 x 13-inch) baking dish or 2 smaller baking dishes. Top with chow mein noodles. Bake for 50 minutes. Serves 8 to 10.

TIP: If you make 2 smaller casseroles, you can freeze one. Wait to sprinkle the chow mein noodles over the casserole until just before you place it in the oven to bake.

Sweet Peach Pork Tenderloin

**3 tablespoons (45 g)
   Dijon-style mustard
1 tablespoon (15 ml) soy
   sauce
340 g (12 ounces) peach
   jam
2 450-g (1-pound) pork
   tenderloins**

- Preheat oven to 160° C (325° F).

- Combine mustard, soy sauce and peach jam in saucepan. Heat and stir just until mixture blends.

- Place pork in sprayed baking pan and spoon peach mixture over top.

- Sprinkle a little salt and pepper over pork.

- Cover pan with foil and bake for 1 hour.

- Remove from oven and let stand for about 10 minutes before slicing. Serves 8.

Pork Chop Dinner

**1 500-g (18-ounce) package
   pork chops
Canola oil
300 ml (12 ounces) pork
   gravy
¼ cup (60 ml) milk
1 425-g (15-ounce) can small
   new potatoes**

- Brown pork chops in large frypan with a little oil. Pour gravy and milk into frypan and stir mixture around chops until they mix well.

- Add new potatoes around chops. Place lid on frypan and simmer on medium-low heat for about 15 minutes or until potatoes are tender. Serves 6.

TIP: The 500-g (18-ounce) package pork chops will give you about 5 to 6 chops if they are of average size.

Sweet Potato Ham

1 450-g (16-ounce) 1-cm (½-inch) thick, fully cooked ham slice

500 g (18 ounces) cooked sweet potatoes

½ cup (110 g) packed brown sugar

⅓ cup (40 g) chopped pecans

- Preheat oven to 175° C (350° F).

- Cut outer edge of ham fat at 2-cm (1-inch) intervals to prevent curling, but do not cut into ham.

- Place on 25-cm (10-inch) microwave-safe dish and grill with top 13 cm (5 inches) from heat for 5 minutes.

- Mash each piece of sweet potato in bowl with fork just once (do not mash completely) and add brown sugar, a little salt and chopped pecans and mix well.

- Spoon mixture over ham slice and return to oven for about 15 minutes. Serves 6.

When buying a ham, the terms 'water added' and 'natural juices added' mean that you are paying for the water weight added to the ham.

Pork Chop Casserole

6 2-cm (¾-inch) thick
   boneless pork
   chops
2 tablespoons (30 ml) canola
   oil
1 green capsicum
1 yellow capsicum,
   seeded and chopped
1 425-g (15-ounce) jar
   tomato simmer sauce
1 425-g (15-ounce) can
   Italian tomatoes
1 teaspoon minced
   garlic
1½ cups (280 g) long grain
   rice

- Preheat oven to 175° C (350° F).

- Sprinkle pork chops with about ½ teaspoon each of salt and pepper. Brown pork chops in oil in frypan. Remove chops from frypan and set aside.

- Cut top off green capsicum, remove seeds, cut 6 rings from green capsicum and set aside. Combine yellow capsicum, simmer sauce, tomatoes, 1 cup (250 ml) water, garlic and ½ teaspoon salt in separate bowl and stir well.

- Spread rice in sprayed 23 x 33-cm (9 x 13-inch) baking dish and slowly pour tomato mixture over rice. Arrange pork chops over rice and place pepper ring over each chop. Cover and bake for 1 hour or until chops and rice are tender. Serves 6.

Easy Pork Stew

This is great with dumplings!

2 450-g (1-pound) pork
    tenderloins, cubed
680 ml (24 ounces) pork
    gravy
¼ cup (70 g) chilli sauce
450 g (16 ounces) frozen stew
    vegetables, thawed

- Cook pork in sprayed soup pot
  on medium-high heat for
  10 minutes, stirring frequently.

- Stir in gravy, chilli sauce and
  stew vegetables and bring
  to a boil. Reduce heat and
  simmer for 12 minutes or until
  vegetables are tender. Serves 4.

Parmesan Covered Pork Chops

½ cup (50 g) grated parmesan
    cheese
⅔ cup (80 g) Italian seasoned
    breadcrumbs
1 egg
4–5 thin-cut pork chops
Canola oil

- Combine cheese and
  breadcrumbs in shallow bowl.
  Beat egg with 1 teaspoon water
  on shallow plate.

- Dip each pork chop in beaten
  egg then into breadcrumb
  mixture.

- Cook over medium-high heat in
  frypan with a little oil for about
  5 minutes on each side or until
  golden brown. Serves 4 to 5.

Marinated Garlic-Herb Tenderloin

2 450-g (1-pound) pork
   tenderloins
1 340-g (12-ounce) bottle
   roasted garlic-herb
   marinade, divided
230 g (8 ounces) fettuccini
   (egg noodles)
¼ cup (60 g) butter

- Butterfly pork lengthwise, being careful not to cut all the way through. Press open to flatten and place in large resealable plastic bag. Pour ¾ cup (190 g) marinade into bag and close top securely. Marinate for 25 minutes and turn several times.

- Grill 10 cm (4 to 5 inches) from heat for 8 minutes.

- Turn pork over and brush with additional marinade and cook for an additional 8 minutes.

- Cook pasta according to package directions with butter. When ready to serve place pork chops over pasta. Serves 8.

*Heating a fully cooked ham is the best way
to bring out the flavours and tenderness.*

Pork Chops with Borlotti Bean Salsa

2 teaspoons chilli powder
2 tablespoons (30 ml) canola oil
6 boneless thin-cut pork chops
1 425-g (15-ounce) can borlotti beans, rinsed and drained
680 g (24 ounces) citrus fruit segmented
1 ripe avocado, sliced
⅔ cup (165 ml) Italian salad dressing

- Combine chilli powder and ½ teaspoon salt in bowl. Rub oil over pork chops and rub chilli powder mixture over chops.

- Place in frypan over medium heat and cook pork chops for about 5 minutes on both sides.

- Combine beans, fruit and avocado in bowl and toss with salad dressing. Serve with pork chops. Serves 6.

Be careful not to overcook thin pork chops.
Cook slowly over medium to low heat.

Onion-Smothered Pork Chops

6 1-cm (½-inch) thick pork chops
1 tablespoon (15 ml) canola oil
2 tablespoons (30 ml) butter
1 onion, chopped
1 280-g (10-ounce) can French onion soup
Brown rice, cooked

- Preheat oven to 160° C (325° F).

- Brown pork chops in oil in frypan, simmer for about 10 minutes and place pork chops in sprayed shallow baking pan.

- Add butter to same frypan and sauté onion. (Pan juices are brown from pork chops so onions will be brown.)

- Add onion soup and ½ cup (125 ml) water and stir well.

- Pour onion soup mixture over pork chops.

- Cover and bake for 40 minutes and serve over brown rice. Serves 6.

You should trim about ½ to 1 cm (¼ to ½ inch) off the fat on the outside of a ham before you spread the glaze on it.

Pork-Potato Chop

**6 boneless or loin pork
    chops**
Canola oil
**400 ml (14 ounces)
    chicken stock**
**2 30-g (1-ounce) packets
    onion soup mix**
**4 new (red) potatoes,
    sliced**

- Season pork chops with a little
  salt and pepper and brown in
  large frypan with a little oil.
  Combine chicken stock and
  soup mix in bowl. Add potatoes
  to frypan with pork chops and
  cover with soup mixture.

- Heat to boil, cover and simmer
  for 45 minutes or until pork
  chops and potatoes are fork-
  tender. Serves 6.

Pork Chops and Gravy

**6 1-cm (½-inch) thick pork
    chops**
**8–10 new (red)
    potatoes with
    peel, quartered**
450 g (16 ounces) baby carrots
**2 280-g (10-ounce) cans
    cream of mushroom
    soup**

- Sprinkle a little salt and pepper
  on pork chops.

- Brown pork chops in frypan and
  place in 5 to 6-L (5 to 6-quart)
  slow cooker. Place potatoes and
  carrots around pork chops.

- Heat mushroom soup with ½ cup
  (125 ml) water in saucepan and
  pour over chops and vegetables.

- Cover and cook in slow cooker
  on low for 6 to 7 hours.
  Serves 6.

Pork Chops, Potatoes and Green Beans

6–8 boneless or loin
  pork chops
300 ml (11 ounces) pork gravy
2 425-g (15-ounce) cans white
  potatoes, drained
2 425-g (15-ounce) cans sliced
  green beans, drained

- Season pork chops with salt and pepper, if desired, and brown pork chops in large non-stick heavy pan over medium heat.

- Pour gravy over pork chops. Cover and simmer for 30 minutes.

- Add potatoes and green beans and simmer for about 10 minutes or until pork chops are tender and green beans and potatoes are hot. Serve with tossed green salad. Serves 6.

Slow-Cooked Ham and Rice

200 g (7 ounces) mixed brown
  and wild rice
2 teaspoons Oriental seasoning
3–4 cups (420–560 g) cooked
  chopped or cubed
  ham
150 g (5 ounces) sliced
  mushrooms
280 g (10 ounces)
  frozen green peas
2 cups (200 g) chopped celery

- Combine rice, seasoning, ham, mushrooms, peas, celery and 2⅔ cups (650 ml) water in 4 to 5-L (4 to 5-quart) slow cooker. Stir to mix well.

- Cover and cook in slow cooker on low for 2 to 4 hours. Serves 6.

Ham-It-Up Dinner

This is really simple to put together and the kids will be ready to eat their vegetables when ham and cheese are in the picture.

1 170-g (6-ounce) package
   long-grain and wild
   rice mix
280 g (10 ounces) frozen
   broccoli florets,
   thawed
1 230-g (8-ounce) can
   corn, drained
3 cups (420 g) cooked, cubed
   ham
1 280-g (10-ounce) can cream
   of mushroom soup
1 cup (225 g) mayonnaise
1 teaspoon mustard
1 cup (115 g) shredded cheddar
   cheese
85 g (3 ounces) onion,
   finely sliced and fried
   until crispy

- Preheat oven to 175° C (350° F).

- Prepare rice according to package directions.

- Spoon into sprayed 3-L (3-quart) baking dish. Top with broccoli, corn and ham.

- Combine soup, mayonnaise, mustard, shredded cheese and ½ teaspoon each of salt and pepper in saucepan and mix well. Spread over top of rice-ham mixture.

- Cover and bake for about 30 minutes. Uncover and sprinkle onion over bake for additional 15 minutes or until casserole is bubbly around the edges and onion is light brown. Serves 8.

TIP: What a great way to use leftover ham; all the little slivers and chunks left from those nice big slices.

Fruit-Covered Ham Slice

2 425-g (15-ounce) cans
   fruit salad, with juice
½ cup (110 g) packed brown
   sugar
2 tablespoons (25 g)
   cornflour
1 1-cm (½-inch) thick
   centre-cut ham
   slice

- Combine fruit salad, brown sugar and cornflour in saucepan and mix well. Cook on medium heat, stirring frequently, until sauce thickens.

- Place ham slice in large non-stick frypan on medium heat. Cook for about 5 minutes or just until ham thoroughly heats.

- Place on serving platter and spoon fruit sauce over ham. Serves 8.

Peach-Glazed Ham

1 2.3-kg (5-pound) boneless ham
450 g (16 ounces) peach jam
3 tablespoons (45 g) Dijon-style
   mustard
¼ cup (55 g) packed brown
   sugar

- Cook ham according to package directions. Combine jam, mustard and brown sugar in bowl and mix well.

- About 30 minutes before cooking time ends, remove ham from oven and drain any liquid.

- Brush ham with jam-and-sugar mixture and return to oven for 30 minutes.

- Heat remaining jam-and-sugar mixture in saucepan. Serve ham with heated mixture. Serves 8.

Pasta and Ham with Veggies

230 g (8 ounces) fettuccini
  (egg noodles)
1 280-g (10-ounce) can cream
  of celery soup
1 280-g (10-ounce) can cream
  of broccoli soup
1 teaspoon chicken
  stock powder
1½ cups (375 ml) unthickened
  cream
1 230-g (8-ounce) can
  corn, drained
1 450-g (16-ounce) package
  frozen broccoli florets,
  cauliflower and
  carrots, thawed
3 cups (420 g) cooked, cubed ham
230 g (8 ounces) shredded
  cheddar cheese

- Preheat oven to 175° C (350° F).

- Cook pasta according to package directions and drain.

- Combine soups, chicken stock, cream, corn, frozen vegetables, ham, ½ teaspoon salt and 1 teaspoon pepper in large bowl and mix well.

- Fold in pasta and half cheese. Spoon into sprayed 23 x 33-cm (9 x 13-inch) baking dish. Cover and bake for 45 minutes.

- Uncover and sprinkle remaining cheese over top of casserole. Return to oven and bake for additional 5 minutes or until cheese is bubbly. Serves 8.

Ham and Potatoes Olé

1 680-g (24-ounce) package
  frozen hash browns,
  thawed and shredded
3 cups (420 g) cooked, cubed
  ham
1 280-g (10-ounce) can cream
  of chicken soup
200 g (7 ounces) processed
  cheese spread
1½ cups (400 g) hot salsa
230 g (8 ounces) shredded
  cheddar cheese

- Preheat oven to 175° C (350° F).

- Combine potatoes, ham, soup,
  cheese and salsa in large bowl
  and mix well. Spoon into
  sprayed 23 x 33-cm
  (9 x 13-inch) baking dish.

- Cover and bake for 40 minutes.
  Uncover and sprinkle cheese
  over casserole and bake for
  additional 5 minutes. Serves 8.

Dinner in a Dish

2 255-g (9-ounce) packages
  boil-in-the-bag rice
3 cups (420 g) cooked, cubed
  ham
1½ cups (170 g) shredded
  cheddar cheese
1 230-g (8-ounce) can green
  peas, drained

- Preheat oven to 175° C (350° F).

- Prepare rice according to
  package directions. Combine
  rice, ham, cheese and peas in
  large bowl.

- Pour into 3-L (3-quart)
  baking dish and bake for
  15 to 20 minutes. Serves 6.

Tortellini-Ham Dinner

This is another great recipe for leftover ham.

2 250-g (9-ounce) packages
    refrigerated tortellini
280 g (10 ounces) frozen green
    peas, thawed
1 450-g (16-ounce) jar
    alfredo sauce
3 cups (420 g) cooked, cubed
    ham

- Cook pasta according to package directions. Add green peas for about 5 minutes before pasta is done and drain.

- Combine alfredo sauce and ham in saucepan and heat until thoroughly hot. Toss with pasta and peas. Serve immediately. Serves 6 to 8.

Ham and Sweet Potatoes

¼ cup (60 g) Dijon-style
    mustard
1 1.4–1.8-kg (3–4-pound)
    boneless smoked
    ham
½ cup (170 g) honey or
    ½ cup (110 g) packed brown
    sugar
700 g (25 ounces) sweet potatoes,
    cooked

- Preheat oven to 160° C (325° F).

- Spread half mustard on ham. Place ham in sprayed shallow baking pan and bake for 20 minutes.

- Combine remaining mustard with honey or brown sugar in bowl and spread over ham. Add sweet potatoes and bake for 20 minutes. Serves 6.

Grilled Ham with Sweet Potatoes

1 1-cm (½-inch) thick fully
  cooked, centre-cut
  ham slice
350 g (12 ounces) sweet
  potatoes, cooked
½ cup (110 g) packed brown
  sugar
2 tablespoons (30 g) butter,
  melted
1 teaspoon ground cinnamon

- Cut edges of ham fat at 2.5-cm
  (1-inch) intervals to prevent
  curling. Place ham on griller tray
  and grill for about 5 minutes.

- Spoon sweet potatoes into
  shallow dish, mash with fork
  and stir in brown sugar, butter
  and cinnamon.

- Spoon sweet potato mixture
  over ham and place under griller.
  Grill for about 5 minutes or until
  sweet potatoes are hot, brown
  and tender. Serves 4 to 6.

Ham and Veggies

2 425-g (15-ounce) cans
  mixed vegetables
1 280-g (10-ounce) can
  cream of celery soup
2 cups (280 g) cooked, cubed
  ham
½ teaspoon dried basil

- Cook vegetables according to
  package directions. Add soup,
  ham and basil.

- Cook until mixture heats well
  and serve hot. Serves 6.

Bow-Tie Pasta with Ham and Veggies

This is a great way to use leftover ham.

230 g (8 ounces) farfalle (bow-tie) pasta

280 g (10 ounces) frozen broccoli florets, thawed

280 g (10 ounces) frozen green peas, thawed

1 450-g (16-ounce) jar alfredo sauce

450 g (1 pound) cooked, cubed ham

- Cook pasta according to package directions in large saucepan. Add broccoli and peas during last 3 minutes of cooking time. Drain well.

- Add alfredo sauce and ham. Cook and stir gently over very low heat to keep ingredients from sticking to pan. Pour into serving bowl. Serves 6 to 8.

German-Style Ribs and Sauerkraut

**1.4–1.8 kg (3–4 pounds)
pork ribs, trimmed
3 potatoes, peeled and
cubed or sliced
1 900-g (32-ounce) jar
sauerkraut, drained
¼ cup (30 g) pine nuts, toasted**

- Brown ribs on all sides in large, sprayed heavy pan. Add a little pepper and 1 cup (250 ml) water. Bring to a boil, reduce heat and simmer for 2 hours or until ribs are very tender.

- Add potatoes and cook on low heat for 20 minutes. Add sauerkraut and continue cooking until potatoes are done.

- Sprinkle pine nuts on ribs and sauerkraut immediately before serving. Serves 6 to 8.

TIP: To toast pine nuts, place nuts in pan on medium heat, and stir constantly, until golden brown. You may also put them on a baking tray and cook at 150° C (300° F) for 5 to 10 minutes.

*Always save a ham bone for soups, stews and beans.
If you don't need it immediately, just freeze it for later.*

Oven-Roasted Pork Ribs

⅓ cup (85 ml) orange juice
⅓ cup (85 ml) soy sauce
1 teaspoon ground
    cumin
½ cup (110 g) packed brown
    sugar
900–1400 g (2–3 pounds)
    pork ribs

• Combine orange juice, soy
  sauce, cumin and brown sugar
  in large resealable plastic bag.
  Shake or mash bag to blend
  thoroughly and to dissolve
  brown sugar.

• Cut pork into individual ribs,
  add to bag and marinate for
  1 to 2 hours.

• When ready to bake, preheat
  oven to 160° C (325° F).

• Transfer ribs and marinade to
  shallow baking pan and arrange
  in 1 layer. Ribs should not
  touch.

• Bake for 45 minutes. Remove
  from oven, turn ribs with tongs
  and continue roasting for an
  additional 1 hour.

*When you are frying ham steaks or thick slices, cut slits in the fat
around the edges and the ham will not curl up around the edges.*

Fettuccini Supreme

**450 g (16 ounces)
  fettuccini (egg noodles)**
½ cup (125 ml) pouring cream
½ cup (115 g) butter
½ teaspoon dried basil
1 tablespoon (2 g) dried parsley
2 cups (280 g) cooked, diced ham
**1 cup (100 g) grated parmesan
  cheese**

- Cook pasta according to package directions and drain. Immediately place pasta back into saucepan.

- Add cream, butter, basil, parsley, ham and ¼ teaspoon salt and toss until butter melts. Fold in parmesan cheese, pour into serving bowl and serve hot. Serves 8.

Creamy Potatoes and Ham

**5 medium potatoes, peeled and
  sliced**
1 teaspoon chicken salt
1 onion, chopped
**2 cups (280 g) cooked, cubed
  ham**
**230 g (8 ounces) cubed
  processed cheese**
**200 g (7 ounces) processed
  cheese spread**
½ cup (125 ml) milk

- Layer half each of potatoes, chicken salt, onion, ham and cheese in slow cooker and repeat layer.

- Combine cheese spread and milk in bowl until fairly smooth and pour over potato mixture. Cover and cook on high for 1 hour. Reduce heat to low and cook for 6 to 7 hours. Serves 6.

Hot Pasta Frittata

½ cup (80 g) chopped onion
1 green capsicum,
    seeded and chopped
1 red capsicum, seeded and
    chopped
3 tablespoons (45 g) butter
230 g (8 ounces) spaghetti,
    slightly broken up
    and cooked
1½ cups (170 g) shredded
    mozzarella cheese
5 eggs
½ cup (125 ml) milk
⅓ cup (35 g) grated parmesan
    cheese
1 tablespoon (2 g) basil
1 teaspoon oregano
2 cups (280 g) cooked, diced ham

- Preheat oven to 190° C (375° F).

- Sauté onion and capsicums in butter in frypan over medium heat for about 5 minutes, but do not brown.

- Combine onion-capsicum mixture and pasta in large bowl and toss. Add mozzarella cheese and toss.

- In separate bowl, beat eggs, milk, parmesan cheese, basil, oregano and about ½ teaspoon each of salt and pepper. Add spaghetti mixture and ham and pour into sprayed 23 x 33-cm (9 x 13-inch) baking pan or 2-L (2-quart) baking dish.

- Cover and bake for 10 minutes. Uncover to make sure eggs are set. If not, bake for additional 2 to 3 minutes. Cut into squares and serve. Serves 8.

TIP: *This can be prepared, refrigerated and baked later. Let it get to room temperature before heating.*

Colourful Veggie and Ham Salad

4 cups (285 g) fresh broccoli
   florets
4 cups (400 g) fresh cauliflower
   florets
1 red onion, sliced
115 g (4 ounces) sliced
   black olivess
3 small zucchini, sliced
2 cups (280 g) cooked, chopped
   ham
1 tablespoon (10 g)
   Italian seasoning
1½ cups (375 ml)
   Italian salad dressing
2 tablespoons (30 ml) extra-
   virgin olive oil

- Combine broccoli, cauliflower, onion, olives, zucchini and ham in large bowl and toss.

- Combine seasoning, dressing and olive oil in small bowl and mix well.

- Pour over vegetables and toss to coat. Refrigerate for several hours before serving or make 1 day in advance. Serves 6.

Good vegetable sources of vitamin C are tomatoes, capsicums, broccoli and cauliflower.

Ham Salad I

3 cups (420 g) cooked, chopped ham
1 bunch spring onions with tops, chopped
½ cup (85 g) slivered almonds, toasted
½ cup (65 g) sunflower seeds
2 cups (140 g) chopped fresh broccoli florets
¾ cup (170 g) mayonnaise
Lettuce leaves

- Combine ham, spring onions, almonds, sunflower seeds and broccoli florets in bowl. Toss with mayonnaise and refrigerate. Serve on lettuce leaves. Serves 4.

Ham Salad II

3 cups (420 g) cooked, chopped ham
¾ cup (75 g) chopped celery
1 cup (225 g) cottage cheese, drained
1 cup (100 g) chopped cauliflower florets
1 cup (70 g) chopped broccoli florets
Honey-mustard salad dressing
Lettuce leaves

- Combine ham, celery, cottage cheese, cauliflower and broccoli in bowl, toss with salad dressing and refrigerate. Serve on lettuce leaves. Serves 4.

Vegetable and Ham Chowder

A great recipe for leftover ham.

1 medium potato
2 280-g (10-ounce) cans
    cream of celery soup
400 ml (14 ounces)
    chicken stock
3 cups (420 g) cooked, diced
    ham
1 425-g (15-ounce) can corn
2 carrots, sliced
1 onion, coarsely chopped

1 teaspoon dried basil
1 teaspoon chicken salt
1 teaspoon white pepper
280 g (10 ounces) frozen
    broccoli florets

- Cut potato into 2-cm (1-inch) pieces. Combine all ingredients except broccoli florets in large slow cooker.

- Cover and cook on low for 5 to 6 hours. Add broccoli and ½ teaspoon salt to cooker and cook for additional 1 hour. Serves 4.

Large or firm vegetables like potatoes, onions and carrots cook more slowly than meat. Put these vegetables in the slow cooker first and put the meat on top of them.

Sandwich Soufflé

A fun lunch!

Butter, softened
8 slices white bread
without crusts
4 slices ham
4 slices cheddar cheese
2 cups (500 ml) milk
2 eggs, beaten

- Butter bread on both sides and make 4 sandwiches with ham and cheese. Place sandwiches in sprayed 20-cm (8-inch) square baking dish.

- Beat milk, eggs and a little salt and pepper in bowl. Pour over sandwiches and soak for 1 to 2 hours.

- When ready to bake, preheat oven to 175° C (350° F).

- Bake for 45 to 50 minutes. Serves 4.

Sausage Casserole

450 g (1 pound) pork sausages
2 425-g (15-ounce) cans
kidney beans
1 425-g (15-ounce) can
tomatoes
1 tablespoon chopped coriander
1 tablespoon lemon juice
1 170-g (6-ounce) package
scone mix
1 egg
⅓ cup (85 ml) milk

- Preheat oven to 205° C (400° F).

- Brown sausages in frypan and drain fat. Add beans, tomatoes, coriander and lemon juice, blend and bring to a boil.

- Pour into sprayed 3-L (3-quart) baking dish. Prepare scone mix with egg and milk in bowl. Drop teaspoonfuls of mixture over meat-bean mixture.

- Bake for 30 minutes or until top is brown. Serves 6.

Loaded Potatoes

6 large baking potatoes, washed
450 g (1 pound) pork sausage mince
230 g (8 ounces) cubed processed cheese
1 280-g (10-ounce) can diced tomatoes
50 g green chillies, sliced

- Cook potatoes in microwave until done. Brown sausage pork in frypan over medium heat and drain fat. Add cheese, tomatoes and green chillies and stir well.

- With knife, cut potatoes down centre and fluff insides with fork.

- Spoon generous amounts of pork-cheese mixture on each potato and reheat in microwave for 2 to 3 minutes, if necessary. Serves 6.

Italian Sausage and Ravioli

450 g (1 pound) Italian pork sausages
1 740-g (26-ounce) jar extra chunky mushroom spaghetti sauce
570 g (20 ounces) package cheese-filled ravioli, cooked and drained
Grated parmesan cheese

- Remove casing from sausages and cook in large frypan over medium heat until brown on the outside and no longer pink in the middle. Stir to separate sausage meat and drain. Stir in spaghetti sauce and heat to boiling.

- Cook pasta according to package directions and add to spaghetti and sausage. Sprinkle with parmesan cheese and pour into serving dish. Serves 6 to 8.

244

365 Easy One-Dish Recipes

Pork-Stuffed Eggplant

1 large eggplant
340 g (¾ pound) minced pork
230 g (½ pound) pork sausages
1 egg
½ cup (60 g) seasoned
    breadcrumbs
½ cup (50 g) grated romano
    cheese
1 tablespoon (2 g) dried
    parsley flakes
1 tablespoon (10 g) dried onion
    flakes
1 teaspoon dried oregano
1 425-g (15-ounce) can
    tomatoes
1 230-g (8-ounce) jar tomato
    simmer sauce

- Preheat oven to 175° C (350° F).

- Cut stem off eggplant and cut in half lengthwise. Scoop out and reserve centre, leaving a 1-cm (½-inch) shell.

- Steam shell halves for about 5 minutes or just until tender. Drain well. Cube reserved eggplant and cook in saucepan with boiling salt water for about 6 minutes, drain well and set aside.

- Cook pork mince and sausages in frypan over medium heat until no longer pink and drain. Add eggplant, egg, breadcrumbs, cheese, parsley flakes, onion flakes, oregano, about ½ teaspoon each of salt and pepper and mix well.

- Fill shells and place in sprayed 18 x 28-cm (7 x 11-inch) baking dish. Pour tomatoes and simmer sauce over eggplant. Cover and bake for 30 minutes. Serves 6.

Sausage and Beans

1 450-g (1-pound) fully cooked smoked, link salami
2 425-g (15-ounce) cans baked beans
1 425-g (15-ounce) can cannellini beans, drained
1 425-g (15-ounce) can borlotti beans, drained
½ cup (135 g) chilli sauce
⅔ cup (150 g) packed brown sugar
1 tablespoon (15 ml) Worcestershire sauce

- Cut salami into 2-cm (1-inch) slices. Layer salami and beans in slow cooker.

- Combine chilli sauce, brown sugar, a little black pepper and Worcestershire sauce in bowl and pour over beans and salami.

- Cover and cook in slow cooker on low for 4 hours. Stir before serving. Serves 8.

You can buy salami in several forms: fresh, cured, cooked, uncooked and dried. Read the labels carefully for cooking instructions.

Perfect Penne

450 g (1 pound) Italian sausages,
    cut into 1-cm (½-inch) chunks
1 onion, cut into long
    strips
1 green capsicum,
    seeded and julienned
1 tablespoon (15 ml) canola oil
1 425-g (15-ounce) can diced
    tomatoes
1 425-g (15-ounce) can Italian
    tomatoes
2 tablespoons (50 g) tomato paste
455 g (16 ounces) penne
    pasta
1 cup (115 g) shredded
    mozzarella cheese

- Preheat oven to 175° C (350° F).

- Cook sausages, onion and capsicum in oil in large frypan over medium heat and drain. Add diced tomatoes, Italian tomatoes and tomato paste and mix well.

- Cook pasta according to package directions and drain. Combine sausage-onion mixture and tomato mixture in large bowl and toss with pasta and cheese. Spoon into sprayed 3-L (3-quart) baking dish. Cover and bake for 20 minutes. Serves 8.

Pizza Pies

230 g (½ pound) pork mince
⅔ cup (170 g) pizza sauce
280 g (10 ounces) refrigerated
  puff pastry sheets
½ cup (60 g) shredded
  mozzarella cheese

- Preheat oven to 205° C (400° F).

- Brown pork in frypan and stir to break up pieces of meat. Drain fat, add pizza sauce and heat until bubbly.

- Cut 6 10-cm (4-inch) squares from the pastry.

- Divide mince mixture evenly among squares and sprinkle with cheese. Lift one corner of each square and fold over filling to make triangle.

- Press edges together with tines of fork to seal. Bake for about 12 minutes or until light golden brown. Serve immediately. Serves 6.

TIP: Use this short-cut version of pizza or put your favourite ingredients inside – I like 'double cheese' on mine, but check your refrigerator for extras. (Additional ingredients may need to be cooked before adding.)

As-Easy-as-Falling-Off-a-Log Baked Ham

Yes, it really is that easy! The best part is that people will rave about it and want to know your recipe.

1 1.8–2.3 kg (4–5 pound) leg or hindquarter ham

- Preheat oven to 175° C (350° F).

- Unwrap plastic wrapping around ham and place in large roasting pan. Wrap foil over top and seal edges around pan opening.

- Bake for 3 to 3½ hours. Remove foil, place ham on large platter and slice. Serves 8.

TIP: This isn't the prettiest cut of pork in the supermarket, but it's very tasty. When you have sliced the meat off the bone, you have great bone and meat scraps for stock.

Easy Baked Chops

4 1-cm (½-inch) pork chops
Canola oil
1–2 tablespoons (15–30 ml) onion soup mix
2 tablespoons (30 ml) French salad dressing

- Preheat oven to 175° C (350° F).

- Brown pork chops on both sides in large frypan with a little oil. Sprinkle soup mix over top.

- Pour in salad dressing and ¼ cup (60 ml) water. Cover and bake for about 1 hour. Serves 4.

Seaworthy Seafood

Hooked, Caught and in the Pan

Seaworthy Seafood Contents

No-Noodle Tuna

230 g (8 ounces)
  refrigerated
  puff pastry sheets
1 cup (115 g) shredded
  cheddar cheese
280 g (10 ounces)
  frozen chopped
  broccoli florets, thawed
4 eggs, beaten
1 60-g (2-ounce) box cream
  of chicken soup mix
230 g (8 ounces) sour cream
1 cup (250 ml) milk
½ cup (110 g) mayonnaise
2 tablespoons (5 g) dried
  onion flakes
½ teaspoon dill
2 170-g (6-ounce) cans
  white meat tuna,
  drained and flaked
1 60-g (2-ounce) jar diced
  roasted red capsicum

- Preheat oven to 175° C (350° F).

- Line a 23 x 33-cm (9 x 13-inch) baking dish with puff pastry.

- Seal seams and sprinkle with cheese and chopped broccoli.

- Combine eggs, chicken soup mix, sour cream, milk, mayonnaise, onion flakes and dill in bowl and mix well. Stir in tuna and roasted red capsicums. Pour over broccoli-cheese in baking dish.

- Cover and bake for 40 minutes or until knife inserted in centre comes out clean. Cut into squares to serve. Serves 8.

Ever-Ready Tuna Casserole

**200 g (7 ounces)
  elbow macaroni**
**230 g (8 ounces)
  shredded processed
  cheese**
**2 170-g (6-ounce) cans
  tuna, drained**
**1 280-g (10-ounce) can
  cream of celery
  soup**
1 cup (250 ml) milk

- Preheat oven to 175° C (350° F).

- Cook pasta according to package directions. Drain well, add cheese and stir until cheese melts.

- Add tuna, celery soup and milk and continue stirring. Spoon into sprayed 18 x 28-cm (7 x 11-inch) baking dish. Cover and bake for 35 minutes or until bubbly. Serves 6.

Tuna-Stuffed Tomatoes

4 large tomatoes
**2 170-g (6-ounce) cans
  white meat tuna,
  drained**
2 cups (200 g) chopped celery
**½ cup (70 g) chopped
  cashews**
**1 small zucchini with peel,
  finely chopped**
½ cup (110 g) mayonnaise

- Cut thin slice off top of each tomato, scoop out flesh and discard. Turn tomatoes top down on paper towels to drain.

- Combine tuna, celery, cashews, zucchini, mayonnaise and a little salt and pepper in bowl and mix well. Spoon mixture into hollowed-out tomatoes. Refrigerate. Serves 4.

Tuna and Asparagus Pot Pie

230 g (8 ounces) refrigerated
   puff pastry
1 170-g (6-ounce) can solid
   white tuna in water,
   drained
1 425-g (15-ounce) can cut
   asparagus, drained
1 cup (115 g) shredded cheddar
   cheese

- Preheat oven to 190° C (375° F).

- Form an 18-cm (7-inch) square of pastry and place in sprayed 20 x 20-cm (8 x 8-inch) square baking pan.

- Spread pastry with tuna, then asparagus and cheese. Form remaining pastry into a square and place on top of cheese.

- Bake for 20 minutes or until top browns and cheese bubbles. Serves 4.

Tubular pastas are hollow, tube-like shapes that come in many different lengths and diameters. Elbow macaroni is an example of 'tube' pasta.

Cannaroni	wide tubes
Cannelloni	large tubes used for stuffing
Ditali	very short tubes
Gigantoni	very large tubes used for stuffing
Manicotti	very large tubes used for stuffing
Mostaccioli	'little moustaches'; smooth tubes
Penne	small tubes cut diagonally
Rigatoni	large tubes with ridges on outside
Tubetti	very small tubes

Ever-Ready Sauce for Tuna

1 tablespoon (15 ml) olive oil
2 teaspoons minced garlic
2 teaspoons sugar
¼ teaspoon cayenne
    pepper
2 teaspoons dried basil
1 425-g (15-ounce) can
    tomatoes
1 340-g (12-ounce) can water-
    packed tuna, drained
¾ cup (95 g) pitted green olives,
    sliced
¼ cup (30 g) drained capers
1 cup (165 g) pasta, cooked

- Heat olive oil in saucepan and add garlic, sugar, cayenne pepper and basil. Cook on low heat for 2 minutes.

- Add tomatoes, bring to a boil, reduce heat and simmer for 20 minutes.

- Combine tuna, olives, capers and pasta in bowl, stir in sauce and toss. Serves 6.

Pasta needs a lot of water to cook properly. Use at least two litres for every 500 grams of dried pasta.

Tuna-in-the-Straw

**230 g (8 ounces) tagliatelle
(egg noodles)
2 280-g (10-ounce) cans
cream of chicken soup
230 g (8 ounces) sour cream
1 teaspoon Cajun
seasoning
½ cup (125 ml) milk
2 170-g (6-ounce) cans white
meat tuna, drained
and flaked
1 cup (115 g) shredded
processed cheese
280 g (10 ounces) frozen
green peas, thawed
1 60-g (2-ounce) jar diced
roasted red capsicum
1 small potato, grated**

- Preheat oven to 175° C (350° F).

- Cook pasta according to package directions and drain. Combine soup, sour cream, Cajun seasoning and milk in large saucepan and mix well.

- Add noodles, tuna, cheese, peas and roasted red capsicum to saucepan. Pour into sprayed 23 x 33-cm (9 x 13-inch) baking dish. Sprinkle grated potato on top.

- Bake for about 35 minutes or until potato is light brown. Serves 6.

Alfredo Salmon and Pasta

3 cups (285 g) fettuccini
   (egg noodles)
450 g (16 ounces) frozen
   broccoli florets, thawed
1 cup (270 g) alfredo sauce
1 425-g (15-ounce) can salmon,
   drained and boned

- Cook pasta in large saucepan according to package directions. Add broccoli during last 5 minutes of cooking time and drain.

- Stir in alfredo sauce and salmon and cook on low heat, stirring occasionally, until mixture heats through. Pour into serving bowl. Serves 6.

TIP: You can make the alfredo sauce yourself, buy it fresh in the refrigerated section of the grocery store or buy it in a jar.

Pan-Fried Flounder

1 tablespoon (15 g) plus
   1 teaspoon salt-and-pepper
   seasoning
¼ teaspoon cayenne pepper
⅔ cup (80 g) flour
¼ cup (60 ml) olive oil
6–8 small flounder fillets
¾ cup (170 g) tartare sauce
⅓ cup (90 g) tomato sauce

- Combine 1 tablespoon (15 g) seasoning, cayenne pepper, flour, ¼ teaspoon pepper and ½ teaspoon salt in bowl.

- Heat oil over high heat in large frypan. Dredge each fillet in flour-seasoning mixture and place in frypan (in batches). Fry for about 3 minutes on each side, depending on thickness of fillets. Drain on paper towels.

- Combine tartare sauce, tomato sauce and 1 teaspoon seasoning in bowl and serve with fried flounder. Serves 6.

Sunday Best Fried Fish

1 450-g (16-ounce) package
  cooked, frozen
  battered fish
1 cup (250 g) spaghetti sauce
2 teaspoons Italian
  seasoning
1 cup (115 g) shredded
  mozzarella cheese

- Heat fish according to package
  directions. While fish is heating,
  combine spaghetti sauce and
  Italian seasoning in bowl.

- When fish heats thoroughly,
  place each piece on serving plate
  and spoon spaghetti mixture
  over fish. Sprinkle cheese on top
  and serve. Serves 6.

Grilled Red Snapper

2 tablespoons (50 g) Dijon-style
  mustard
¼ cup (60 ml) Italian salad
  dressing
4 170-g (6-ounce) red
  snapper fillets

- Preheat griller. Combine
  mustard and Italian dressing
  in small bowl.

- Place snapper, skin-side
  down, on sprayed, foil-lined
  baking pan.

- Brush mustard-dressing mixture
  over fillets and grill for about
  8 minutes or until snapper flakes
  easily when tested with fork.
  Serves 4.

Grilled Swordfish with Pepper Sauce

4 2-cm (1-inch) swordfish steaks
3 tablespoons (45 ml) olive oil
¾ teaspoon seasoned salt
½ teaspoon lemon pepper
⅓ cup (40 g) roasted red capsicum
1 tablespoon (15 g) Dijon-style mustard
3 tablespoons (35 g) mayonnaise

• Rub swordfish with olive oil and sprinkle with seasoned salt and lemon pepper.

• Grill over medium-high heat for about 10 minutes, turning once or until it cooks thoroughly. (Do not overcook, as this will dry fish out.)

• Place roasted red capsicum, mustard, mayonnaise and ½ teaspoon pepper in blender and process until they blend well. Serve over grilled swordfish. Serves 4.

The most important thing to remember about cooking fish is not to overcook it. The internal temperature should be about 60° C (145° F) and the flesh should be opaque. Don't let fish dry out.

Extra Special Fried Fish

1 450-g (16-ounce) package
  cooked, frozen batter-dipped
  fried fish
¾ cup (205 g) chilli sauce
1 bunch spring
  onions, chopped
1 cup (115 g) shredded cheddar
  cheese

- Preheat oven to 160° C (325° F).

- Arrange fish in sprayed
  23 x 33-cm (9 x 13-inch) glass
  baking dish and heat for about
  20 minutes or just until fish
  heats thoroughly.

- Heat chilli sauce in saucepan
  and spoon over each piece of
  fish. Top with spring onions and
  cheddar cheese. Serve right from
  baking dish. Serves 6.

Frypan Prawn Scampi

2 teaspoons olive oil
1 kg (2 pounds) prawns, peeled,
  veined
⅔ cup (150 ml) herb-garlic
  marinade with lemon
  juice
¼ cup (25 g) finely chopped
  spring onions with tops
Rice or pasta, cooked

- Heat oil in large non-stick
  frypan. Add prawns and
  marinade and cook, stirring
  often, until prawns turn pink.

- Stir in spring onions. Serve over
  rice or pasta. Serves 6.

Red Snapper with Fresh Salsa

6 170-g (6-ounce) red
    snapper fillets
Canola oil
1 teaspoon ground
    cumin
½ teaspoon cayenne
    pepper
½ cup (10 g) chopped fresh
    coriander
1 425-g (15-ounce) can
    cannellini beans, drained
1 425-g (15-ounce) can Italian
    tomatoes, drained
⅓ cup (45 g) chopped green
    olives
1 teaspoon minced garlic

- Dry snapper with paper towels and rub a little oil on both sides of snapper. Sprinkle with cumin, cayenne pepper and ½ teaspoon salt.

- Grill snapper for about 5 minutes on each side or until fish flakes easily when tested with fork.

- Combine coriander, beans, tomatoes, olives and garlic in bowl and mix well. Serve with each red snapper and garnish with slice of fresh lime, if you like. Serves 6.

Salmon and Green Beans

Canola oil
4 170-g (6-ounce) salmon
    steaks
¼ cup (60 ml) light soy sauce
2 tablespoons (30 ml) lemon
    juice
280 g (10 ounces) frozen
    whole green beans
Rice, cooked

- Place a little oil in frypan over medium-high heat and add salmon steaks. Combine soy sauce and lemon juice in bowl and pour over steaks.

- Cover and cook for about 5 minutes. Turn salmon and place green beans over salmon with 2 tablespoons (30 ml) water.

- Cover and steam for 5 minutes or until beans are tender but crisp. Season green beans with a little salt and pepper and serve over rice. Serves 4.

Even with the high content of fats in some species of salmon, all salmon are rated highly for their protein, B-group vitamins, vitamin A and Omega-3 oils.

Salmon Casserole

1 170-g (6-ounce) package
linguine (egg noodles)
1 280-g (10-ounce) can cream
of celery soup
1 145-g (5-ounce) can
evaporated milk
1 tablespoon (15 ml) lemon juice
½ onion, chopped
1 425-g (15-ounce) can salmon,
skin removed, boned
1 cup (115 g) shredded cheddar
cheese
1 230-g (8-ounce) can small
green peas, drained
½ teaspoon seasoned salt
¼ teaspoon white pepper
½ teaspoon Cajun seasoning
1 cup (60 g) crushed cheese
crackers
2 tablespoons (30 g) butter,
melted

• Preheat oven to 175° C (350° F).

• Cook pasta according to package directions and drain.

• Stir in soup, evaporated milk, lemon juice, onion, salmon, cheese, peas, seasoned salt, white pepper and Cajun seasoning. Spoon into sprayed 18 x 28-cm (7 x 11-inch) baking dish. Cover and bake for 25 minutes.

• Combine cheese crackers and butter in bowl and sprinkle over casserole. Return to oven for 10 minutes or until crumbs are light brown. Serves 8.

Thai Prawn and Peanut Noodles

1 150-g (5½-ounce) packet Thai rice noodles with seasoning packet
450 g (1 pound) peeled, veined prawns
280 g (10 ounces) frozen broccoli florets, thawed
Canola oil
½ cup (75 g) peanuts

- Boil 3 cups (750 ml) water in saucepan and stir in noodles. Turn heat off and soak noodles for about 5 minutes. Drain and rinse in cold water.

- Sauté prawns and broccoli in frypan with a little oil for about 8 minutes or just until prawns turn pink.

- Add softened noodles, seasoning packet and peanuts. (There may be chopped peanuts in the seasoning, but this dish is better if you add more peanuts.) Serves 6.

TIP: If noodles are still too firm after they soak, add 1 tablespoon (15 ml) water and stir-fry until noodles are tender.

Prawns are available in hundreds of varieties, but they can generally be divided between warm-water prawns and cold-water prawns. As a general rule, cold-water prawns are smaller, but more succulent. All varieties range in colour from deep red, pink, white and grey to green. Most change colour when cooked.

Savoury Prawn Fettuccini

2 tablespoons (30 g) butter
⅓ cup (55 g) chopped onion
1 teaspoon salt-and-pepper
   seasoning
230 g (½ pound) small prawns,
   peeled and veined
1 280-g (10-ounce) can seafood
   bisque soup
½ cup (125 ml) unthickened
   cream
½ cup (110 g) mayonnaise
2 teaspoons Worcestershire sauce
½ teaspoon horseradish
1 cup (115 g) shredded
   cheddar cheese
230 g (8 ounces) fettuccini
   (egg noodles), cooked
450 g (16 ounces) frozen
   broccoli florets, cooked

- Preheat oven to 175° C (350° F).

- Melt butter in large saucepan and sauté onion. Add seasoning and prawns and cook, stirring, until prawns turn pink, about 2 minutes.

- Add soup, cream, mayonnaise, Worcestershire sauce, horseradish and half cheese. Heat just until cheese melts. Fold in pasta.

- When broccoli cools from cooking, fold into sauce.

- Spoon into sprayed 3-L (3-quart) baking dish. Cover and bake for 30 minutes.

- Remove from oven and sprinkle remaining cheese on top and bake for additional 5 minutes. Serves 8.

Fettuccini Marinara

¼ cup (60 g) butter
¼ cup (30 g) flour
1 teaspoon Cajun seasoning
¾ teaspoon white pepper
1 tablespoon (15 g) minced
    garlic
500 ml (16 ounces) unthickened
    cream
½ cup (125 ml) milk
½ cup (75 g) finely chopped
    red capsicum
2 170-g (6-ounce) cans tiny
    prawns, veined
2 170-g (6-ounce) cans
    crabmeat, picked and
    drained
1 170-g (6-ounce) can
    chopped clams, drained

½ cup (50 g) grated
    parmesan cheese
340 g (12 ounces) fettuccini
    (egg noodles), cooked
    al dente
Parsley

- Preheat oven to 160° C (325° F).

- Melt butter in saucepan and add
  flour, Cajun seasoning, white
  pepper and garlic and mix well.
  On medium heat, gradually add
  cream and milk and mix well.
  Cook, stirring constantly until
  the mixture thickens.

- Add capsicum, prawns,
  crabmeat, clams and parmesan
  cheese and heat thoroughly.
  Spoon half pasta and half
  seafood sauce into sprayed
  23 x 33-cm (9 x 13-inch) baking
  dish. Repeat layers.

- Cover and bake for 25 minutes
  or just until casserole is bubbly.
  To serve, sprinkle parsley over
  top of casserole. Serves 8.

Crab-Stuffed Baked Potatoes

This potato dish is truly a meal in itself!

4 large baking potatoes
½ cup (115 g) butter
½ cup (125 ml) pouring cream
1 bunch spring onions, chopped
2 170-g (6-ounce) cans crabmeat, drained and flaked
¾ cup (85 g) shredded cheddar cheese
2 tablespoons (20 g) fresh minced parsley

• Preheat oven to 190° C (375° F).

• Bake potatoes for 1 hour or until well done. Halve each potato lengthwise and scoop out flesh, but leave skins intact.

• Mash potato flesh with butter in large bowl. Add cream, ¾ teaspoon salt, ½ teaspoon pepper and spring onions. Stir in crabmeat.

• Fill reserved potato skins with potato mixture. Sprinkle with cheese. Bake at 175° C (350° F) for about 15 minutes. To serve, sprinkle fresh parsley over cheese. Serves 4.

Russet potatoes are ideal for baking and are also called baking potatoes or Idaho potatoes. Their starch content makes these excellent for baking, frying and boiling.

No-Panic Crab Casserole

2 170-g (6-ounce) cans
crabmeat, drained and
flaked
1 cup (125 ml) unthickened
cream
1½ cups (335 g) mayonnaise
6 eggs, hard-boiled and
finely chopped
1 cup (120 g) seasoned
breadcrumbs
1 tablespoon (2 g) dried
parsley flakes
½ teaspoon dried basil
1 230-g (8-ounce) can sliced
water chestnuts, drained
2 tablespoons (30 g) butter,
melted

- Preheat oven to 175° C (350° F).

- Combine crabmeat, cream, mayonnaise, eggs, ½ cup (60 g) seasoned breadcrumbs, parsley, basil, water chestnuts and a little salt and pepper in bowl and mix well.

- Pour into sprayed 2-L (2-quart) baking dish.

- Combine remaining breadcrumbs and butter and sprinkle over top of casserole.

- Bake for 40 minutes. Serves 6.

Creamed Prawns over Rice

3 280-g (10-ounce) cans
 seafood bisque soup
500 ml (1 pint) sour cream
1½ teaspoons curry powder
2 170-g (6-ounce) cans
 prawns, veined
Rice, cooked

- Combine all ingredients in double boiler. Heat and stir constantly but do not boil.

- Serve over rice. Serves 4.

Prawn Newburg

1 280-g (10-ounce) can
 seafood bisque soup
1 teaspoon seafood
 stock powder
450 g (1 pound) cooked, veined
 prawns
Rice, cooked

- Combine soup, ¼ cup (60 ml) water and seafood stock in saucepan. Bring to a boil, reduce heat and stir in prawns.

- Heat thoroughly and serve over rice. Serves 6.

Approximate Prawn Quantities per Kilogram

Prawns (jumbo)	*25–34 per kilogram*
Extra Large	*35–44 per kilogram*
Large	*45–70 per kilogram*
Medium	*71–80 per kilogram*
Small	*81–100 per kilogram*

Prawns in Sour Cream

2 spring onions, chopped
230 g (8 ounces) fresh
  mushrooms, cleaned
  and sliced
2 tablespoons (30 g) butter
450 g (1 pound)
  prawns, cooked,
  peeled and cleaned
1 tablespoon (10 g) flour
1 teaspoon Worcestershire
  sauce
2 tablespoons (30 ml) dry sherry
230 g (8 ounces) sour cream
Rice, cooked

- Sauté spring onions and mushrooms in butter in frypan for 5 minutes.

- Add prawns and heat. Sprinkle mixture with flour, Worcestershire sauce and ½ teaspoon each of salt and pepper. Add sherry and sour cream, mix well.

- Cook over low heat until hot, but do not allow to boil. Serve over rice. Serves 8.

In general, 1 kilogram of uncooked prawns will yield about 750 grams of cooked prawns.

Prawn Scampi

½ cup (115 g) butter
3 cloves garlic, pressed
¼ cup (60 ml) lemon juice
Tabasco sauce
1 kg (2 pounds) prawns, peeled

• Melt butter in frypan, sauté
  garlic and add lemon juice and a
  few dashes of Tabasco sauce.

• Arrange prawns in single
  layer in shallow pan. Pour
  garlic-butter over prawns and
  salt lightly.

• Grill for 2 minutes, then turn
  and grill for additional
  2 minutes. Reserve garlic butter
  and serve separately. Serves 6.

Orange Roughy with Capsicum

450 g (1 pound) orange roughy
    fillets
Canola oil
1 onion, sliced
2 red capsicums, julienned
1 teaspoon dried thyme leaves
¼ teaspoon black pepper

• Cut fish into 4 serving-size
  pieces. Heat a little oil in frypan.
  Layer onion and capsicum and
  sprinkle with half thyme and
  pepper.

• Place fish over capsicum and
  sprinkle with remaining thyme
  and pepper.

• Turn burner on high until fish
  is hot enough to cook. Lower
  heat, cover and cook fish for
  15 to 20 minutes or until fish
  flakes easily. Serves 6.

Neptune Lasagna

3 tablespoons (45 g) butter
1 red capsicum, chopped
1 onion, chopped
230 g (8 ounces) cream cheese,
   softened
1½ cups (340 g)
   cottage cheese
1 egg, beaten
2 teaspoons dried basil
2 teaspoons Cajun
   seasoning
1 280-g (10-ounce) can
   seafood bisque soup
1 280-g (10-ounce) can cream
   of celery soup
½ cup (125 ml) white wine
¾ cup (175 ml) milk
2 230-g (8-ounce) packages
   imitation crabmeat
230 g (8 ounces) cooked, peeled,
   veined prawns
9 lasagna sheets, cooked and
   drained
⅓ cup (35 g) grated parmesan
   cheese
1 cup (115 g) shredded
   cheddar cheese

- Preheat oven to 175° C (350° F).

- Heat butter in frypan and sauté capsicum and onion. Reduce heat, add cream cheese and stir until cream cheese melts. Remove from heat and add cottage cheese, egg, 2 teaspoons basil, ½ teaspoon pepper and Cajun seasoning and set aside.

- Combine soups, white wine, milk, crabmeat and prawns in bowl and mix well.

- Arrange 3 lasagna sheets in sprayed 23 x 33-cm (9 x 13-inch) baking dish. Spread with one-third of cottage cheese mixture and one-third seafood mixture. Repeat layers twice. Sprinkle with parmesan cheese.

- Cover and bake for about 40 minutes.

- Uncover and sprinkle with cheddar cheese and bake for additional 10 minutes or until casserole bubbles. Let stand for at least 15 minutes before serving. Serves 8 to 10.

No Ordinary Prawn

½ cup (160 g) chopped onion
1 red capsicum, thinly
    sliced
5 tablespoons (75 g) butter,
    divided
2 tablespoons (15 g) flour
¾ cup (175 ml) unthickened
    cream
1 teaspoon Worcestershire sauce
3 cups (420 g) cooked, peeled,
    veined prawns
2 cups (560 g) cooked white rice
¾ cup (85 g) shredded cheddar
    cheese
¾ cup (45 g) round buttery
    cracker crumbs

- Preheat oven to 175° C (350° F).

- Sauté onion and capsicum in
  3 tablespoons (45 g) butter in
  frypan, but do not brown.

- Blend in flour, ½ teaspoon
  each of salt and pepper, heat and
  mix well.

- On medium heat, gradually add
  cream and Worcestershire sauce
  and stir until broth thickens.
  Fold in prawns.

- Place cooked rice in sprayed
  18 x 28-cm (7 x 11-inch) baking
  dish and spread out. Pour prawn
  mixture over rice.

- Sprinkle cheese over top and
  combine cracker crumbs and
  remaining melted butter in bowl.
  Sprinkle over casserole.

- Bake for about 20 to 25 minutes
  or until crumbs are light brown.
  Serves 8.

BONUS!
Desserts

Cold, Hot,
Creamy, Crispy
and Yummy

BONUS! Desserts Contents

Sweet Angel Cake

This will get rave reviews when it's served.

1½ cups (180 g) icing sugar
⅓ cup (75 ml) milk
230 g (8 ounces) cream cheese,
    softened
100 g (3½ ounces) flaked
    coconut
1 cup (110 g) chopped pecans
340 g (12 ounces) pouring cream
1 large angel-food cake,
    torn into bite-size pieces
1 455-g (16-ounce) can cherry
    pie filling

- Add icing sugar and milk to cream cheese and beat in bowl.

- Fold in coconut and pecans, stir in cream and cake pieces.

- Spread in 23 x 33-cm (9 x 13-inch) glass dish and refrigerate for several hours.

- Add pie filling by the tablespoon on top of cake mixture. (It will not completely cover cake mixture, but it will just be in clumps, making a pretty red and white dessert.)

- Refrigerate. Serves 15 to 16.

Coloured Sugar

You can easily make your own coloured sugar to use on biscuits and cakes by adding a few drops of food colouring and mixing well until all the sugar is coated. Add 2 drops to ¼ cup sugar.

Chocolate Hurricane Cake

This is easy and very, very yummy.

1 cup (110 g) chopped pecans
85 g (3 ounces) dessicated
coconut
1 500-g (18-ounce) box rich
chocolate cake mix
⅓ cup (75 ml) canola oil
3 eggs
½ cup (115 g) butter, melted
230 g (8 ounces) cream cheese,
softened
450 g (16 ounces) icing sugar

- Preheat oven to 175° C (350° F).

- Cover bottom of sprayed, floured 23 x 33-cm (9 x 13-inch) baking tray with pecans and coconut.

- Combine cake mix, 1¼ cups (310 ml) water, oil and eggs in bowl and beat well. Carefully pour batter over pecans and coconut.

- Combine butter, cream cheese and icing sugar in bowl and whip to blend. Spoon mixture over unbaked batter and bake for 40 to 42 minutes. Serves 18.

TIP: You cannot test if this cake is ready with a skewer because it will appear sticky even when it is done. The icing sinks into the bottom as it bakes and forms a white ribbon inside.

Turtle Cake WOW!

**1 500-g (18-ounce) box rich
    chocolate cake mix
½ cup (115 g) butter,
    softened
½ cup (125 ml) canola oil
1 400-g (14-ounce) can sweetened
    condensed milk
1 450-g (1-pound) bag caramels
1 cup (110 g) chopped pecans**

- Preheat oven to 175° C (350° F).

- Combine cake mix, butter,
  1½ cups (375 ml) water, oil
  and half sweetened condensed
  milk. Pour half batter into
  sprayed, floured 23 x 33-cm
  (9 x 13-inch) baking tray and
  bake for 20 minutes.

- Melt caramels and blend with
  remaining sweetened condensed
  milk. Spread evenly over baked
  cake layer and sprinkle with
  pecans. Cover with remaining
  batter and bake for an additional
  20 to 25 minutes.

Icing:

**½ cup (115 g) butter
3 tablespoons (30 g) cocoa
6 tablespoons (90 ml) evaporated
    milk
450 g (16 ounces) icing sugar
1 teaspoon vanilla**

- Melt butter in saucepan and mix
  in cocoa and milk. Add icing
  sugar and vanilla to mixture and
  blend well. Spread over cake.
  Serves 24.

Coconut Cake Deluxe

This cake is really moist and delicious and can be frozen if you need to make it in advance.

1 500-g (18-ounce) box batter cake mix
1 400-g (14-ounce) can sweetened condensed milk
1 425-g (15-ounce) can coconut cream
85 g (3 ounces) dessicated coconut
230 g (8 ounces) whipped cream

- Preheat oven to 175° C (350° F).

- Prepare cake mix according to package directions and pour into sprayed, floured 23 x 33-cm (9 x 13-inch) baking tray.

- Bake for 30 to 35 minutes or until toothpick inserted in centre comes out clean. While cake is warm, punch holes in cake about 5 cm (2 inches) apart.

- Pour sweetened condensed milk over cake and spread around until all milk soaks into cake. Pour coconut cream over cake and sprinkle coconut on top. Cool and ice with whipped cream. Serves 12 to 15.

Easy Breezy Pineapple Cake

2 cups (400 g) sugar
2 cups (240 g) flour
1 570-g (20-ounce) can crushed
   pineapple with juice
1 teaspoon bicarbonate of soda
1 teaspoon vanilla

- Preheat oven to 175° C (350° F).

- Combine all cake ingredients and ½ teaspoon salt in bowl and mix well with spoon.

- Pour into sprayed, floured 23 x 33-cm (9 x 13-inch) baking pan and bake for 30 to 35 minutes. Ice while hot.

Icing:

230 g (8 ounces) cream cheese,
   softened
½ cup (115 g) butter,
   melted
1 cup (120 g) icing sugar
1 cup (110 g) chopped pecans

- Beat all ingredients except pecans in bowl.

- Add pecans, stir to mix well and spread over hot cake. Serves 12.

Apply icing with a metal spatula to get a nice smooth finish. (If you're using an icing that's somewhat thick, you can also dip your spatula in hot water to warm it, then wipe the water off. This will make smoothing the icing over the cake easier.)

Chocolate Biscuit Cake

1 500-g (18-ounce) box butter
  cake mix
⅓ cup (75 ml) canola oil
4 egg whites
1¼ cups (75 g) coarsely crushed
  chocolate biscuits

- Preheat oven to 175° C (350° F).

- Combine cake mix, 1¼ cups
  (310 ml) water, oil and egg
  whites in large bowl. Blend
  on low speed until moist. Beat
  for 2 minutes on high speed
  and gently fold in coarsely
  crushed biscuits.

- Pour batter into 2 sprayed,
  floured 20 or 23-cm
  (8 or 9-inch) cake tins and bake
  for 25 to 30 minutes or until
  toothpick inserted in centre
  comes out clean. Cool for
  10 minutes, remove from pan
  and cool completely.

Icing:

4¼ cups (510 g) icing sugar
1 cup (230 g) butter,
  softened
1 cup (190 g) shortening (not
  butter)
1 teaspoon almond
  flavouring
¼ cup (15 g) crushed chocolate
  biscuits
¼ cup (30 g) chopped pecans

- Beat all ingredients except
  crushed biscuits and pecans
  in bowl. Ice first layer, place
  second layer on top and ice top
  and sides. Sprinkle crushed
  biscuits and pecans on top.
  Serves 20.

*TIP: Butter is not the best
    shortening for this recipe, so
    use an unflavoured shortening
    instead, if possible.*

Pina Colada Cake

1 500-g (18-ounce) box orange
   cake mix
3 eggs
⅓ cup (75 ml) canola oil
1 400-g (14-ounce) can
   sweetened condensed
   milk
1 425-g (15-ounce) can coconut
   cream
1 cup (85 g) dessicated coconut
1 230-g (8-ounce) can crushed
   pineapple, drained
230 g (8 ounces)
   whipped cream

- Preheat oven to 175° C (350° F).

- Combine cake mix, eggs,
  1¼ cups (310 ml) water and oil
  in bowl. Beat for 3 or 4 minutes
  and pour into sprayed, floured
  25 x 38-cm (10 x 15-inch)
  baking tray.

- Bake for 35 minutes. When cake
  is done, punch holes in cake
  with fork so icing will soak into
  cake.

- Mix sweetened condensed milk,
  coconut cream, coconut and
  pineapple in bowl. While cake is
  warm, pour mixture over cake.
  Refrigerate until cake is cold,
  spread whipped cream over cake
  and return to refrigerator.
  Serves 22.

Chocolate-Cherry Cake

**1 500-g (18-ounce) box
chocolate cake mix
1 570-g (20-ounce) can cherry
pie filling
3 eggs**

- Preheat oven to 175° C (350° F).

- Combine cake mix, pie filling
and eggs in bowl and mix
with spoon. Pour into sprayed,
floured 23 x 33-cm (9 x 13-inch)
baking dish.

- Bake for 35 to 40 minutes. Cake
is done when toothpick inserted
in centre comes out clean.

- Spread icing over hot cake.

Icing:

**5 tablespoons (75 g) butter
1¼ cups (250 g) sugar
½ cup (125 ml) milk
170 g (6 ounces) chocolate chips**

- When cake is almost done,
combine butter, sugar and milk
in medium saucepan. Boil for
1 minute, stirring constantly.
Add chocolate chips and stir
until chips melt. Pour over hot
cake. Serves 20.

*Semi-sweet and sweet baking chocolate, which comes
in chips, bars or squares, contains between
15 and 35% chocolate liquor plus sugar and vanilla.*

Hawaiian Dream Cake

1 500-g (18-ounce) box butter cake mix
4 eggs
¾ cup (175 ml) canola oil
280 g (10 ounces) crushed pineapple with juice

- Preheat oven to 175° C (350° F).

- Beat all ingredients in bowl for 4 minutes.

- Pour into sprayed, floured 23 x 33-cm (9 x 13-inch) baking tray.

- Bake for 30 to 35 minutes or until toothpick inserted in centre comes out clean. Cool and pour icing over cake.

Icing:

280 g (10 ounces) crushed pineapple with juice
½ cup (115 g) butter
450 g (16 ounces) icing sugar
170 g (6 ounces) dessicated coconut

- Heat pineapple and butter in saucepan and boil for 2 minutes.

- Add icing sugar and coconut.

- Punch holes in cake with knife and pour hot icing over cake. Serves 20.

Pecan Pie

2 tablespoons (15 g) flour
3 tablespoons (45 g) butter, melted
3 eggs, beaten
⅔ cup (135 g) sugar
1 cup (250 ml) corn syrup*
1 teaspoon vanilla
1 cup (110 g) chopped pecans
1 sheet of frozen shortcrust
    pastry, thawed

- Preheat oven to 175° C (350° F).

- Combine flour, butter, eggs,
  sugar, corn syrup and vanilla in
  bowl and mix well.

- Line a greased 23-cm (9-inch)
  pie dish with shortcrust pastry.
  Place pecans in piecrust and
  pour egg mixture over pecans.

- Bake for 10 minutes, then reduce
  heat to 140° C (275° F) and bake
  for 50 to 55 minutes or until centre
  of pie is fairly firm. Serves 8.

*TIP: Corn syrup can be bought
    from your local delicatessen
    if you can't find it at the
    supermarket.

Creamy Lemon Pie

230 g (8 ounces) cream cheese,
    softened
1 400-g (14-ounce) can
    sweetened condensed
    milk
¼ cup (60 ml) lemon juice
570 g (20 ounces) lemon
    butter
1 sheet of frozen shortcrust
    pastry, thawed

- Beat cream cheese in bowl
  until smooth and creamy. Add
  sweetened condensed milk
  and lemon juice and beat until
  mixture is creamy.

- Fold in lemon butter and stir
  until mixture blends well. Line
  a greased 23-cm (9-inch) pie
  dish with shortcrust pastry.
  Pour filling into piecrust and
  refrigerate for several hours
  before slicing and serving.
  Serves 8.

Kahlua Pie

26 marshmallows
340 ml (12 ounces)
**   evaporated milk**
30 g (1 ounce)
**   unflavoured gelatine**
250 ml (8 ounces)
**   pouring cream**
½ cup (125 ml) Kahlua
1 sheet frozen shortcrust
**   pastry, thawed**
Chocolate curls

- Melt marshmallows with evaporated milk in saucepan over medium-low heat. Stir constantly and do not let milk boil.

- Dissolve gelatine in ¼ cup (60 ml) cold water. Remove marshmallow mixture from heat and add dissolved gelatine. Refrigerate until mixture thickens slightly.

- Whip cream and fold into marshmallow mixture. Mix in Kahlua. Line a greased 23-cm (9-inch) pie dish with shortcrust pastry and pour filling into piecrust. Garnish with chocolate curls and refrigerate overnight. Serves 8.

Why are pie dishes round? In the past, housewives literally cut corners to stretch the ingredients. This is also why pie dishes are shallow.

Dream Pie

**230 g (8 ounces)
cream cheese,
softened
1 400-g (14-ounce) can
sweetened
condensed milk
1 145-g (5-ounce) package
vanilla instant
pudding mix
230 g (8 ounces) whipped cream
2 sheets frozen shortcrust
pastry, thawed
570 g (20 ounces) tinned berries**

- Beat cream cheese and sweetened condensed milk in bowl until smooth.

- Add pudding mix and ½ cup (125 ml) water, mix and refrigerate for 15 minutes.

- Fold in whipped cream. Line 2 greased 23-cm (9-inch) pie dishes with pastry, pour filling into dishes and freeze.

- When ready to serve, remove from freezer and place in refrigerator for 45 minutes before slicing and serving.

- Spoon about ¼ cup (65 g) tinned berries on each slice of pie. Serves 16.

TIP: For a change, you can also pour 2 or 3 tablespoons (20 to 25 ml) chocolate topping over pie and top with chocolate shavings.

Peach-Mousse Pie

450 g (16 ounces) drained tinned
     peach slices
1 cup (200 g) sugar
30 g (1 ounce) unflavoured
     gelatine
⅛ teaspoon ground
     nutmeg
A few drops yellow
     food colouring
A few drops red
     food colouring
340 g (12 ounces) whipped cream
1 sheet frozen shortcrust
     pastry, thawed

- Place peaches in blender and process until smooth. Pour into saucepan, bring to a boil and stir constantly. Remove from heat.

- Combine sugar, gelatine and nutmeg in bowl and stir into hot puree until sugar and gelatine dissolve. Pour gelatine mixture into large bowl and place in freezer for 20 minutes or until mixture mounds. Stir occasionally.

- Beat gelatine mixture on high speed for 5 minutes or until light and fluffy. Add colouring, fold in whipped cream and pour into a greased 23-cm (9-inch) pie dish lined with shortcrust pastry. Serves 8.

Outta-Sight Pie

1 400-g (14-ounce) can
    sweetened condensed milk
570 g (20 ounces)
    lemon butter
1 570-g (20-ounce) can
    crushed pineapple,
    drained
230 g (8 ounces)
    whipped cream
2 sheets frozen shortcrust
    pastry, thawed

- Combine sweetened condensed milk, lemon butter and pineapple in saucepan over medium-low heat and mix well. Allow to cool.

- Fold in whipped cream and pour mixture into 2 greased pie dishes lined with shortcrust pastry. Refrigerate for several hours before serving. Serves 16.

Sweet Potato Pie

425 g (15 ounces) sweet
    potatoes, cooked
¾ cup (175 ml) milk
1 cup (220 g) packed brown
    sugar
2 eggs
½ teaspoon ground
    cinnamon
1 sheet frozen shortcrust
    pastry, thawed

- Preheat oven to 175° C (350° F).

- Combine all ingredients plus ½ teaspoon salt in bowl and blend until smooth.

- Line a greased 23-cm (9-inch) pie dish with pastry and fill with sweet-potato mixture.

- Bake for 40 minutes or until knife inserted in centre comes out clean. (Shield edges of pastry with aluminium foil to prevent excessive browning.) Serves 6.

Apricot Cobbler

This is another one of those recipes that is really quick and easy plus really delicious.

**1 570-g (20-ounce) can apricot
pie filling
1 570-g (20-ounce) can crushed
pineapple with juice
1 cup (110 g) chopped pecans
1 500-g (18-ounce) box butter
cake mix
1 cup (230 g) butter, melted
Whipped cream**

- Preheat oven to 175° C (375° F).

- Pour apricot pie filling into sprayed, floured 23 x 33-cm (9 x 13-inch) baking tray and spread evenly.

- Spoon crushed pineapple and juice over pie filling. Sprinkle pecans over pineapple, then sprinkle cake mix over pecans.

- Pour butter over cake mix and bake for 40 minutes or until light brown and crunchy. To serve, top with whipped cream. Serves 10.

Pecans contain no cholesterol and add essential fibre, vitamin E, magnesium, thiamine and copper to the diet. They are also high in monounsaturated fats that help lower LDL cholesterol levels.

Seven-Layer Slice

½ cup (115 g) butter
1 cup (100 g) crushed plain sweet
  biscuits
170 g (6 ounces) semi-sweet
  chocolate bits
170 g (6 ounces)
  white chocolate bits
85 g (3 ounces) dessicated
  coconut
1 400-g (14-ounce) can
  sweetened condensed
  milk
1 cup (110 g) chopped pecans

• Preheat oven to 175° C (350° F).

• Melt butter in 23 x 33-cm
  (9 x 13-inch) baking tray.
  Sprinkle remaining ingredients
  in order listed.

• Do not stir or mix. Bake for
  30 minutes. Cool before cutting.
  Serves 15.

Vanishing Butter Biscuits

1 500-g (18-ounce) box butter
  cake mix
1 100-g (3½-ounce) package
  butterscotch instant
  pudding mix
1 cup (250 ml) canola oil
1 egg, beaten
1¼ cups (165 g) chopped pecans

• Preheat oven to 175° C (350° F).

• Mix cake and pudding mixes in
  bowl with spoon and stir in oil.
  Add egg, mix thoroughly and
  stir in pecans.

• Place teaspoonfuls of dough
  on baking tray about 5 cm
  (2 inches) apart.

• Bake for 8 or 9 minutes. Do not
  overcook. Yields 3 dozen.

Easy Blonde Brownies

This is another one of those recipes that seems too easy to be a recipe – and you already have everything in the pantry.

**450 g (16 ounces) light
    brown sugar**
4 eggs
2 cups (240 g) scone mix
2 cups (220 g) chopped pecans

- Preheat oven to 175° C (350° F).

- Beat brown sugar, eggs and scone mix in bowl. Stir in pecans.

- Pour into sprayed 23 x 33-cm (9 x 13-inch) baking tray. Bake for 35 minutes. Cool and cut into squares. Serves 20.

Snappy Treats

3 cups (240 g) quick-cooking oats
1 cup (170 g) chocolate chips
½ cup (85 g) flaked coconut
½ cup (110 g) chopped pecans
2 cups (400 g) sugar
¾ cup (170 g) butter
½ cup (125 ml) evaporated milk

- Combine oats, chocolate chips, coconut and pecans in large bowl.

- Boil sugar, butter and milk in saucepan for 1 to 2 minutes and stir constantly.

- Pour hot mixture over oat-chocolate mixture in bowl and stir until chocolate chips melt.

- Drop teaspoonfuls of mixture onto baking paper. Cool at room temperature and store in covered container. Yields 3 dozen.

*TIP: Use white chocolate chips
    and ¾ cup (130 g) chopped
    glacé cherries for a
    colourful variation.*

Buttery Walnut Squares

1 cup (230 g) butter,
    softened
1¾ cups (385 g) packed brown
    sugar
1¾ cups (180 g) flour

- Preheat oven to 175° C (350° F).
  Combine butter and brown sugar
  in bowl and beat until smooth
  and creamy. Add flour and mix
  well.

- Pat mixture down evenly in
  sprayed 23 x 33-cm
  (9 x 13-inch) baking tray and
  bake for 15 minutes.

Topping:

1 cup (220 g) packed brown
    sugar
4 eggs, lightly beaten
2 tablespoons (15 g) flour
2 cups (260 g) chopped walnuts
1 cup (85 g) dessicated coconut

- Combine brown sugar and eggs
  in medium bowl. Add flour and
  mix well.

- Fold in walnuts and coconut
  and pour over crust. Bake for
  20 to 25 minutes or until set in
  centre. Cool in pan and cut into
  squares. Serves 20.

*TIP: Serve these delicious squares
    with a scoop of ice-cream for
    a great dessert.*

---

*When the recipe says to 'beat' the ingredients, it means to
stir rapidly in a circular motion. You can do this with an electric
mixer (usually set to medium speed) or by hand. One hundred
strokes by hand roughly equals 1 minute by electric mixer.*

Pecan Squares

2 cups (240 g) flour
½ cup (60 g) icing sugar
1 cup (230 g) butter,
   cut up
1 400-g (14-ounce) can
   sweetened condensed
   milk
2 eggs
1 teaspoon vanilla
200 g (7 ounces) toffees, chopped
1 cup (110 g) chopped pecans

- Preheat oven to 175° C (350° F).

- Combine flour and icing sugar in medium bowl and mix well. Cut in butter with pastry blender or fork until crumbly.

- Press mixture evenly into sprayed 23 x 33-cm (9 x 13-inch) baking tray and bake for 15 minutes.

- Combine sweetened condensed milk, eggs, vanilla, toffee bits and pecans in bowl and pour into prepared crust. Bake for 25 minutes or until golden brown.

- Cool and cut into squares. Yields 4 dozen squares.

Hello Dollies

1½ cups (150 g) crushed
  plain sweet biscuits
170 g (6 ounces) chocolate chips
1 cup (85 g) flaked coconut
1¼ cups (140 g) chopped pecans
1 400-g (14-ounce) can
  sweetened condensed
  milk

- Preheat oven to 175° C (350° F).

- Sprinkle crushed biscuits in
  23 x 23-cm (9 x 9-inch) square
  slice tin. Layer chocolate chips,
  coconut and pecans. Pour
  sweetened condensed milk over
  top of layered ingredients.

- Bake for 25 to 30 minutes. Cool
  and cut into squares. Serves 20.

Rocky Road Bars

340 g (12 ounces) semi-sweet
  chocolate chips
1 400-g (14-ounce) can
  sweetened condensed
  milk
2 tablespoons (30 g) butter
2 cups (290 g) dry-roasted
  peanuts
280 g (10 ounces) miniature
  marshmallows

- Place chocolate chips,
  sweetened condensed milk and
  butter in double saucepan. Heat
  until chocolate and butter melt,
  stirring constantly.

- Remove from heat and stir in
  peanuts and marshmallows.

- Spread mixture quickly on
  paper-lined 23 x 33-cm
  (9 x 13-inch) pan. Refrigerate
  for at least 2 hours. Cut into bars
  and store in refrigerator.
  Serves 18.

Lemon-Angel Bars

**1 450-g (1-pound) package
angel food cake mix
570 g (20 ounces) lemon
butter
⅓ cup (75 g) butter, softened
450 g (16 ounces) icing sugar
2 tablespoons (30 ml) lemon juice**

- Preheat oven to 175° C (350° F).
Combine cake mix and lemon
butter in bowl and stir to mix
well.

- Pour into sprayed 23 x 33-cm
(9 x 13-inch) baking tray and
bake for 20 minutes or until
done. Remove cake from oven
just before cake is done.

- Combine butter, icing sugar and
lemon juice in bowl and spread
over hot layer. Cake will sink
down a little in middle, so make
sure frosting is on edges of cake
as well as in middle.

- When cool, cut into 18 to 24 bars
and store in refrigerator. Bars can
be served at room temperature or
cold. Yields 18 to 24 bars.

*Brownies and slices are much easier to remove from the pan
if you line the pan with foil. Here's an easy method. Turn
the pan upside down and cover it with a big enough piece
to cover the sides as well as the bottom of the pan. Be sure to
place the foil shiny side down. Press the foil around the pan,
carefully remove it and turn the pan over. Fit the shaped foil,
shiny side up, into the pan. Use a paper towel to smooth it down.*

Fruit Fajitas

1 570-g (20-ounce) can fruit
    pie filling
10 small flour tortillas
1½ cups (300 g) sugar
¾ cup (170 g) butter
1 teaspoon almond
    flavouring

- Divide fruit equally on tortillas, roll and place in 23 x 33-cm (9 x 13-inch) baking dish. Combine 2 cups (500 ml) water, sugar and butter in saucepan and bring to a boil.

- Add almond flavouring and pour mixture over flour tortillas. Place in refrigerator and let soak for 1 to 24 hours.

- When ready to bake, preheat oven to 175° C (350° F).

- Bake for 20 to 25 minutes until brown and bubbly. Serves 8 to 10.

Chocolate Biscuit Sundae

540 g (19 ounces) chocolate
    biscuits, crushed
½ cup (115 g) butter, melted
2 L (½ gallon) vanilla
    ice-cream, softened
680 g (24 ounces) fudge
    ice-cream topping
340 g (12 ounces)
    whipped cream
Maraschino cherries

- Set aside ½ cup (30 g) biscuit crumbs for topping. Combine remaining crumbs and butter in bowl to form crust. Pour mixture into sprayed 23 x 33-cm (9 x 13-inch) dish and press down.

- Spread softened ice-cream over crust and add layer of fudge sauce. Top with whipped cream and reserved crumbs. Garnish with cherries and freeze until ready to serve. Serves 12.

Lemon Lush

1¼ cups (150 g) flour
⅔ cup (150 g) butter
½ cup (55 g) chopped pecans
1 cup (120 g) icing sugar
230 g (8 ounces) cream cheese,
    softened
340 g (12 ounces) whipped
    cream
2 100-g (3½-ounce)
    packages vanilla instant
    pudding
2 tablespoons (30 ml) lemon
    juice
2¾ cups (425 g) milk

• Preheat oven to 175° C (375° F).

• Combine flour, butter and pecans in bowl and pat down into 23 x 33-cm (9 x 13-inch) baking dish. Bake for 15 minutes.

• Beat icing sugar and cream cheese in bowl until fluffy and fold in 2 cups (150 g) whipped cream. Spread mixture over nut crust.

• In separate bowl, combine instant pudding, lemon juice and milk and beat. Spread over second layer. Top with remaining whipped cream and refrigerate. To serve, cut into squares. Serves 20.

Baked Apples

4–5 large baking apples
1 tablespoon (15 ml) lemon juice
⅓ cup (40 g) dried cranberries
½ cup (55 g) chopped pecans
**¾ cup (165 g) packed brown
  sugar**
**½ teaspoon ground
  cinnamon**
¼ cup (60 g) butter, melted
Caramel ice-cream topping

- Scoop out centre of each apple and leave cavity about 1 cm (½ inch) from bottom.

- Peel top of apples down about 2 cm (1 inch) and brush lemon juice on peeled edges.

- Combine dried cranberries, pecans, brown sugar, cinnamon and butter in bowl. Spoon mixture into apple cavities.

- Pour ½ cup (125 ml) water in slow cooker and place apples on bottom.

- Cover and cook on low for 1 to 3 hours or until tender.

- Serve warm or at room temperature drizzled with caramel ice-cream topping. Serves 5.

Creamy Banana Pudding

*This is a quick and easy
way to make the old
favourite banana pudding.*

**1 400-g (14-ounce) can sweetened
condensed milk**
**1 100-g (3½-ounce) package
instant vanilla
pudding mix**
**230 g (8 ounces)
whipped cream**
36 plain sweet biscuits
3 bananas

- Combine sweetened condensed
milk and 1½ cups (375 ml) cold
water in large bowl.

- Add pudding mix and beat well.

- Refrigerate for 5 minutes and
fold in whipped cream.

- Spoon 1 cup (250 ml) pudding
mixture into 3-L (3-quart)
glass serving bowl. Top with
biscuits, bananas and pudding.
Repeat layers twice and end
with pudding.

- Cover and refrigerate.
Serves 8 to 10.

*Sweetened condensed milk has 50% of the water removed. The
remaining mixture is 40% sugar and is very sticky and sweet.*

Index